An Overview of the *Writers INC SourceBook*

Part I

The Writing Framework

The writing framework offers a variety of real-life writing experiences. Student and professional models are provided for each form of writing, as are step-by-step guidelines.

Part II

Writing Workshops

The writing workshops cover all phases of the writing process—from selecting interesting subjects to organizing writing, from advising in peer groups to editing for clarity.

Part III

Practical Writing

The practical writing section contains writing activities useful both in school and later on the job.

Table of Contents

98

Academic Writing

Part II Writing Workshops

200

Refining: Proofreading

Part III Practical Writing

The Writing Framework

Part I

Grade 9 Activities and Outcomes

The activities in the grade 9 framework provide students with a wide variety of opportunities to re-create and connect past incidents, to describe other people and events, to generate and share creative pieces, to develop essays and personal responses, and to form explanations and summaries.

Personal Writing:

Personal Reminiscence ● Re-create a personal experience from the past.
Related Reminiscences ● Connect past incidents by subject or theme.

Subject Writing:

Description of a Person ● Describe a person so as to create a distinct impression of him or her.
Secondhand Story ● Share a memorable incident in someone else's life.
Eyewitness Account ● Provide a detailed and accurate account of an event you witnessed.
Summary Report from Single Source ● Summarize accurately the contents of a single source of information.

Creative Writing:

Fictionalized Journal Entry ● Write a journal entry.
Character Sketch ● Bring an interesting character to life in a brief descriptive piece.
Memory Poem ● Shape the details of a past event into a poem.
Dialogue Writing ● Generate a believable dialogue.

Reflective Writing:

Essay of Illustration ● Develop an essay in which a personal incident illustrates a generalization.
Dialogue of Ideas ● Generate a dialogue exploring a timely topic.
Response to Reading ● Form a personal response to a literary work.
Pet Peeve ● Present personal feelings about a common, everyday annoyance in a brief personal essay.

Academic Writing:

Essay of Information ● Form a meaningful essay from a list of related facts.
Essay to Explain a Process ● Explain how something works in a step-by-step manner.
*Paragraph Writing ● Generate a series of expository paragraphs.
*The Summary ● Summarize the main ideas of a lecture or a reading selection.

* These extended units, as well as a sequence of letter-writing and on-the-job writing activities, can be found in the Practical Writing section of the SourceBook.

Overview of the Framework Design

Each writing framework is designed to be efficient and user-friendly for both the teacher and student. Each student-guidelines page is presented in a clear, step-by-step fashion. All models contain an introduction and helpful margin notes.

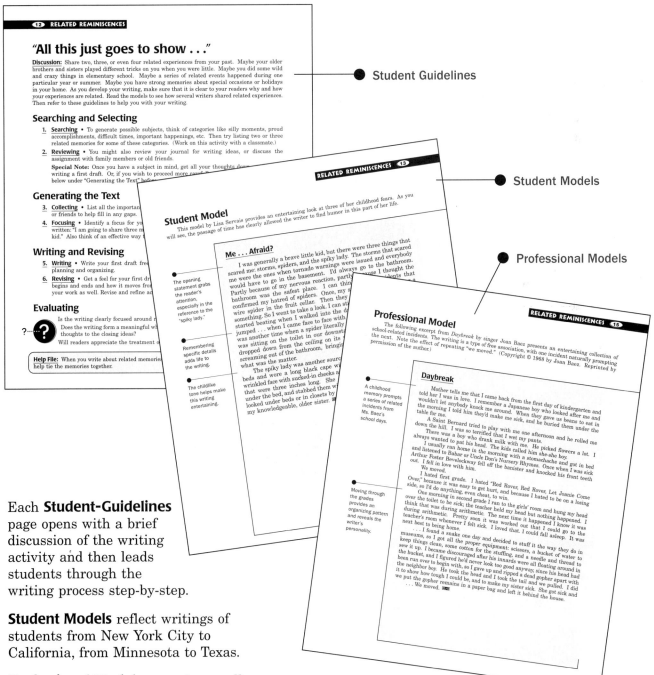

Student Guidelines

Student Models

Professional Models

Each **Student-Guidelines** page opens with a brief discussion of the writing activity and then leads students through the writing process step-by-step.

Student Models reflect writings of students from New York City to California, from Minnesota to Texas.

Professional Models come from well-known authors, as well as journalists.

Personal Writing

"I know I am not capable of suffering more than I did during those few minutes of suspense in the dark, surrounded by those creeping, bloody-minded tarantulas." —Mark Twain

Personal Reminiscence

The personal reminiscence focuses on an incident from the writer's past. By concentrating on specific details, dialogue, and action words, the writer recreates a memorable experience, giving the piece an as-it-happened quality.

From the Beginning . . .

Discussion: Share an unforgettable incident or event from your past that happened over a relatively short period of time. This incident might have taken only a few minutes, or perhaps it extended over a few hours or the better part of a day. You might focus on a thrilling adventure, a silly incident, a serious or solemn event, a frightening few minutes . . . Be sure to include enough specific detail to make your writing come alive for your readers. Provided below are basic guidelines to help you develop your work. Also note the models following these guidelines. Additional information can be found in the handbook. (Refer to "Writing, About an event" in the index.)

Searching and Selecting

1. **Selecting** • You should have little trouble thinking of a subject to write about. You're simply looking for an incident that appeals to you personally and that will have some appeal to your readers.

2. **Reviewing** • Review your journal entries for ideas for your writing. Or focus your attention on a specific time in your past and list related ideas as they come to mind. Then again you might want to talk about the good old days with a friend or classmate.

   Special Note: If the subject of your writing is vivid in your memory, go right to the first draft if you want. Otherwise, follow the guidelines for "Generating the Text."

Generating the Text

3. **Recording** • Write freely about your subject, once you have one in mind, to see how much you already know about it and what you need to find out. (Try writing nonstop for at least 5 minutes.)

4. **Collecting** • Collect additional details if necessary, using the suggestions in the handbook as your guide. (Refer to "Writing, About an Event" for these suggestions.)

5. **Focusing** • State a possible focus or idea you want to express in your writing. Then plan accordingly, selecting and organizing details that support this impression.

Writing and Revising

6. **Writing** • Write your first draft freely, working in details as they naturally come to mind or according to your planning.

7. **Revising** • Carefully review, revise, and refine your writing before sharing it. Remember that your goal is to re-create this incident in living color for your readers. (Refer to the Proofreader's Guide in the handbook when you are ready to proofread your work.)

Evaluating

Is the writing focused around a specific incident or event?

Does the writing contain effective supporting details?

Does the writing sound sincere and honest?

Will readers appreciate the treatment of this subject?

Student Model

Adventure and excitement often come in strange shapes and sizes for children. In the following model, writer Rod Vick recalls the time he learned how to sled in the summer—on a block of ice, no less. Maybe you have a thrill-seeking adventure of your own to share. Read "Ice Blocking" and see how it can be done.

ICE Blocking

The fundamentals of ice blocking are described in the opening paragraph.

I always thought it was impossible to go sledding without snow. But that was before I tried "ice blocking" one warm summer day a few years ago. Some friends, who were experienced in the sport, and I bought six 10-pound blocks of ice from a local gas station. Then we wheeled the heavy blocks in some wagons to the top of a large, grassy hill in a nearby park. I remember the hill being much steeper than I had at first thought. I watched in amazement as my friends held each block in place while the rider laid a towel over the ice before mounting. As soon as the holder let go, the rider was off, moving slowly at first, but quickly picking up speed as the ice began to melt from the friction. One by one, my friends took their turns—slip-sliding their way down the hill. The hill soon turned into a gooey mess which made getting the ice block up the hill seem almost as challenging as the ride down.

The details of the author's first ride are relived in the second paragraph.

It all looked like too much fun to resist, so finally I gathered up the courage to try. It wasn't easy sitting on the ice, but that was nothing compared to controlling the slippery sled as it shot full bore down a hill. I hadn't realized that a block of ice could go so fast and in a path almost entirely of its own making. Near the bottom of my first ride, I hit a major bump and flew off, rolling over and over in the muck. When I came to a stop, I was coated with mud and grass and lucky not to have broken a leg or an arm or something else in the process. ⚉

Student Model

In this model, writer Laura Baginski shares an entertaining incident involving herself (obviously), her mother, and a tomato. Pay special attention to Ms. Baginski's attitude throughout the piece. Does she seem to set herself up for the surprising finish? (This model appeared in the June 1992 commemorative issue of the *High School Writer*, a monthly publication of student writing. It is reprinted with permission.)

Tomato on the Brain

Specific examples of the mother's words of wisdom are provided.

"If you keep crossing your eyes like that, young lady, they'll stay like that and you won't ever get married." My mother was at it again. She went on to say, "It's true. There was a little girl in Bolivia who crossed her eyes just like you do and then it was permanent. She died all alone." Words of wisdom from my all-knowing mother. She seemed to have a lethal warning or terrifying story about anything that gave me the slightest bit of pleasure. "If you keep eating candy like that, your teeth will fall out and then you'll look like those disgusting hillbillies you see on TV."

I never listened to her. I would sit there with my eyes crossed, shoveling chocolate into my mouth just to show her. Defying my mother was a kind of mission for me. She knew this, and it terrified her all the more.

The main focus of the writing is the monkey-bars affair.

One day I was hanging upside down from my knees on my monkey bars. I glanced around the yard. Hanging there, the world was completely rearranged; the trees looked like feather dusters, the basket of vegetables underneath me seemed to replace the clouds, and my dog seemed to be flying. My mother was laboriously caring for her precious yet weed-infested garden. She worked in such jerking, hummingbird-like movements that watching her from an upside-down position was a special and amusing treat.

Wiping sweat off her brow, she peered at me over her shoulder and shook her head. "You know, if you hang upside down like that, all the blood rushing to your brain will make your head blow up."

I smiled. A challenge. This was what I had been waiting for. The sheer excitement of the possibility of my head exploding motivated me to hang there longer.

The writer goes to extremes in describing her dangerous situation.

After five minutes, my temples began to throb. My heart felt like a big lump of pain and seemed to weigh at least 200 pounds. My entire body was numb. I could feel all the blood rushing to my brain like a flash flood. My mother's wise warnings jabbed and replayed over and over in my mind. I was suddenly gripped with the realization that my head was indeed going to blow up.

I tried to get down, but paralysis seized me. In a panic, I closed my eyes and envisioned fragments of my head strewn around the yard. I saw myself transformed into fertilizer for my mother's garden, my severed eyes and nose in my father's tomato patch, dripping off the lilac patch, flowing down the fence. . . .

The drama increases right up to the messy end of the incident.

Suddenly, darkness washed over me and I was falling, sinking . . . until my head struck something offering little resistance. The impact jolted me out of my trance.

As my eyes tried to focus, I reached my hand to my head, checking to see how much of it was left. What my hand discovered was soft, mushy, brainlike. Struck with terror, I brought my trembling hand to my focusing eyes. It was oozing, it was red, it was . . . it was . . . a tomato! 〰

Student Model

In this model personal reminiscence, the student author remembers a painful time in her life. Note that the actual incident covers a very brief period of time, recalled in great detail, almost as if time were standing still. (The author's name has been withheld because of the sensitivity of the subject matter.)

My Mind Went Blank . . .

A dramatic opening immediately grabs the reader's attention.

Most of my first 15 years have been pretty typical, but there is one experience that sticks out above all the others. It changed my life forever.

I was around nine years old and my sisters were ten and seven, and not one of us was old enough to understand what was going on. All we knew was that Dad worked second shift, and that he was rarely home on weekends. While he was at work, my mother would go out, so we really didn't see either of them together very much. When we did, they would do nothing but holler at each other. As one would expect, this was upsetting to children our age, so we often ran to our rooms and pretended not to hear.

The writer focuses her attention on the specific incident as it happened.

As I remember it now, it was a Monday, a day they must have been planning for a long time. My sisters and I had just come home from school, and my dad was waiting inside the door. But he didn't even say hello when we came in. He just said, "As soon as you take off your school clothes, your mother and I would like to talk to you in the front room." We knew something was wrong because my father was home in the middle of the afternoon, and his voice was stern when he spoke to us. We could also see that my mother had been crying.

We changed quickly and quietly, without the usual sisterly squabbling. We were soon in the front room, wrapped around our mother, trying our best to comfort each other. My dad began to talk. "Girls, from now on, I'm going to be home when you get home from school." For a moment I was relieved. Then, he finished, "There will be one other change—your mother will not be living with us any longer." The smile fell from my face. My mind went blank, and I must have gone into a mild case of shock. I remember seeing my sisters crying hysterically, but I couldn't cry. I just stared at my dad. I knew he was talking again, but I couldn't hear what he was saying.

The mother's good-bye is recalled in great detail.

I saw my mother get up and walk toward the door. She had a suitcase in her hand, and my sisters were walking with her. She stopped and gave them a big hug and kiss. But I just stood there and stared. I couldn't kiss her good-bye—I just stood there frozen. I knew she was talking to me, but I couldn't hear anything. I did hear the door close and, like a robot, I walked to the front window. Then as my mother pulled away, the spell was broken, and I began to cry. From then on all I did was cry and wonder why this was happening to me.

The writer puts the experience into perspective for herself and her readers.

In the days and weeks ahead, I slowly adjusted to our new life. I began to realize why certain things happen, why a husband and wife sometimes have to go their separate ways—even when there are children involved. I came to realize that they weren't doing this for strictly selfish reasons, and they certainly didn't want to hurt their children. They knew that continuing to live together would only bring more problems and more hurt to everyone involved. I love them both for all they've done for me and my sisters. Still, I hope my children never have to live through a similar experience. ✍

Professional Model

Mark Twain, the famous author of the following personal reminiscence, is known for many things, including his special brand of homespun humor. As you read the following passage, see if you can find anything comical about it. Do you think Twain himself found anything humorous about this incident? What indications are there that this passage was written a long time ago? (This model is reprinted from *Roughing It* [Signet Classic], the story of Mark Twain's western experiences.)

Tarantulas

A sense of drama and danger are established in the first main paragraph.

"Turn out, boys—the tarantulas is loose!"

No warning ever sounded so dreadful. Nobody tried, any longer, to leave the room, lest he might step on a tarantula. Every man groped for a trunk or a bed, and jumped on it. Then followed the strangest silence—a silence of grisly suspense it was, too—waiting, expectancy, fear. It was as dark as pitch, and one had to imagine the spectacle of those fourteen scant-clad men roosting gingerly on trunks and beds, for not a thing could be seen. Then came occasional little interruptions of the silence, and one could recognize a man and tell his locality by his voice, or locate any other sound a sufferer made by his gropings or changes of position. The occasional voices were not given to much speaking—you simply heard a gentle exclamation of "Ow!" followed by a solid thump, and you knew the gentleman had felt a hairy blanket or something touch his bare skin and had skipped from a bed to the floor. Another silence. Presently you would hear a gasping voice say:

Presenting the spoken words of some of the men adds realism to the writing.

"Su-su-something's crawling up the back of my neck!"

Every now and then you could hear a little subdued scramble and a sorrowful "O Lord!" and then you knew that somebody was getting away from something he took for a tarantula, and not losing any time about it, either. Directly a voice in the corner rang out wild and clear: "I've got him! I've got him!" (Pause, and probable change of circumstances.) "No, he's got me! Oh, ain't they never going to fetch a lantern!"

Take special note of the words Twain uses. What "landscape" is he talking about? What does he mean by "furzy"?

. . . The landscape presented when the lantern flashed into the room was picturesque, and might have been funny to some people, but not to us. Although we were perched so strangely upon boxes, trunks, and beds, and so strangely attired, too, we were too earnestly distressed and too genuinely miserable to see any fun about it, and there was not the semblance of a smile anywhere visible. I know I am not capable of suffering more than I did during those few minutes of suspense in the dark, surrounded by those creeping, bloody-minded tarantulas. I had skipped from bed to bed and from box to box in a cold agony, and every time I touched anything that was furzy I fancied I felt the fangs. I had rather go to war than live that episode over again. . . .

"The spiky lady was another source of fear for me. She lived under beds and wore a long black cape with a big hood." —Lisa Servais

Related Reminiscences

To share related reminiscences, a writer presents a series or cluster of past incidents. The key to this form of writing is to tie the incidents together in an effective and creative way.

"All this just goes to show . . ."

Discussion: Share two, three, or even four related experiences from your past. Maybe your older brothers and sisters played different tricks on you when you were little. Maybe you did some wild and crazy things in elementary school. Maybe a series of related events happened during one particular year or summer. Maybe you have strong memories about special occasions or holidays in your home. As you develop your writing, make sure that it is clear to your readers why and how your experiences are related. Read the models to see how several writers shared related experiences. Then refer to these guidelines to help you with your writing.

Searching and Selecting

1. **Searching** • To generate possible subjects, think of categories like silly moments, proud accomplishments, difficult times, important happenings, etc. Then try listing two or three related memories for some of these categories. (Work on this activity with a classmate.)

2. **Reviewing** • You might also review your journal for writing ideas, or discuss the assignment with family members or old friends.

   Special Note: Once you have a subject in mind, get all your thoughts down on paper by writing a first draft. Or, if you wish to proceed more carefully, follow the guidelines listed below under "Generating the Text" before you attempt a first draft.

Generating the Text

3. **Collecting** • List all the important details related to your memories. Ask family members or friends to help fill in any gaps.

4. **Focusing** • Identify a focus for your work. The author of "Me . . . Afraid?" might have written: "I am going to share three memories about what really scared me when I was a little kid." Also think of an effective way to begin your writing. Plan and organize accordingly.

Writing and Revising

5. **Writing** • Write your first draft freely as thoughts come to mind—or according to your planning and organizing.

6. **Revising** • Get a feel for your first draft by reading it more than once. Do you like how it begins and ends and how it moves from one point to the next? Have a classmate react to your work as well. Revise and refine accordingly.

Evaluating

Is the writing clearly focused around related memories?

Does the writing form a meaningful whole, moving smoothly and clearly from the opening thoughts to the closing ideas?

Will readers appreciate the treatment of the subject?

Help File: When you write about related memories, you must be selective and focus on details that help tie the memories together.

Student Model

This model by Lisa Servais provides an entertaining look at three of her childhood fears. As you will see, the passage of time has clearly allowed the writer to find humor in this part of her life.

Me . . . Afraid?

I was generally a brave little kid, but there were three things that scared me: storms, spiders, and the spiky lady. The storms that scared me were the ones when tornado warnings were issued and everybody would have to go in the basement. I'd always go to the bathroom. Partly because of my nervous reaction, partly because I thought the bathroom was the safest place. I can think of two incidents that confirmed my hatred of spiders. Once, my sister and brother hung a wire spider in the fruit cellar. Then they told me to come and see something. So I went to take a look. I can still remember how my heart started beating when I walked into the dark, little room and how it jumped . . . when I came face to face with that big, ugly spider. There was another time when a spider literally scared the pants off of me. I was sitting on the toilet in our downstairs bathroom when a spider dropped down from the ceiling on its web. I ran bare bunned and screaming out of the bathroom, bringing everyone in the house to see what was the matter.

The spiky lady was another source of fear for me. She lived under beds and wore a long black cape with a big hood. She had a gray, wrinkled face with sucked-in cheeks and sunken eyeballs and fingernails that were three inches long. She grabbed little kids, dragged them under the bed, and stabbed them with her long butcher knives. I never looked under beds or in closets by myself after I heard about her from my knowledgeable, older sister. ✍

The opening statement grabs the reader's attention, especially in the reference to the "spiky lady."

Remembering specific details adds life to the writing.

The childlike tone helps make this writing entertaining.

Student Model

Student writer Kate Keefe freely enjoys the simple things in life, from watching seagulls to receiving simple gifts. As you will see, all of these things relate to special people and places in her life.

The writer opens with a sensitive description of her great-grandmother.

Nothing . . . or Everything?

Today I spent my day with my great-grandmother who is turning one-hundred years old this Monday. Looking at her trunk full of memories, listening to her talk about her childhood and sing her songs, watching her eat the tiny bits of lobster meat that she loves so much, I sit quietly. Her words seep into my heart, and tears fall from my eyes.

I returned home and started to write my English paper, my great-grandmother still in my mind and heart. "If I get something for nothing, does that mean it's worth nothing?" I ask myself. I think back on the day spent with my family. I got something for nothing that day. I received the love of my family, and it was worth more than anything I could ever have bought.

During the summer, when my family is in Maine, I get up every morning and lie on the beach to watch the day begin. As the sun rises over the Atlantic, the seagulls dip over the horizon. I throw scraps of bread to them. They call to let the other gulls know that there is food being offered. The gulls seem to get everything for nothing. Their lives depend on the scraps that strangers throw and the life of the sea around them. They get this for free, and they give pleasure freely to me. . . .

The main part of this reminsicence describes different things received for nothing.

When I am given something for nothing, it is worth the most to me. Once I was given a simple rock from the beach. I carry that stone in my pocket. It symbolizes the unconditional friendship that I have with my friend Pete. I know that whenever I need good advice, Pete is right there by my side. He asks for nothing in return.

Once when walking out of a pizza place, Nicole picked up two withered flowers. She handed one to me and the other to Jess. Jess carelessly threw her flower to the ground. I kept mine, and it still sits on my desk, a keepsake of the fun Nicole and I have had. Next to the flower is a lock of hair given to me this summer by my friend Matt. It reminds me of the trust that Matt and I share.

Like the other keepsakes, written words from family and friends mean more to the writer than they would mean to anyone else.

A personal narrative written about me by my cousin Nifty and the Dada poems of my friend Liam are bonds of writing that I share with these people. A poem from my mother and a letter from my sister remind me of the love of my family. All of my keepsakes were given for nothing, given freely. To a lot of people they might seem worthless. But to me these things are everything. Sometimes, nothing is really everything in life. ✎

Professional Model

The following excerpt from *Daybreak* by singer Joan Baez presents an entertaining collection of school-related incidents. The writing is a type of free association, with one incident naturally prompting the next. Note the effect of repeating "we moved." (Copyright © 1968 by Joan Baez. Reprinted by permission of the author.)

Daybreak

A childhood memory prompts a series of related incidents from Ms. Baez's school days.

Mother tells me that I came back from the first day of kindergarten and told her I was in love. I remember a Japanese boy who looked after me and wouldn't let anybody knock me around. When they gave us beans to eat in the morning I told him they'd make me sick, and he buried them under the table for me.

A Saint Bernard tried to play with me one afternoon and he rolled me down the hill. I was so terrified that I wet my pants.

There was a boy who drank milk with me. He picked flowers a lot. I always wanted to pat his head. The kids called him she-she boy.

I usually ran home in the morning with a stomachache and got in bed and listened to Babar or Uncle Don's Nursery Rhymes. Once when I was sick Arthur Foster Bevelockway fell off the banister and knocked his front teeth out. I fell in love with him.

We moved.

I hated first grade. I hated "Red Rover, Red Rover, Let Joanie Come Over," because it was easy to get hurt, and because I hated to be on a losing side, so I'd do anything, even cheat, to win.

Moving through the grades provides an organizing pattern and reveals the writer's personality.

One morning in second grade I ran to the girls' room and hung my head over the toilet to be sick; the teacher held my head but nothing happened. I think that was during arithmetic. The next time it happened I know it was during arithmetic. Pretty soon it was worked out that I could go to the teacher's room whenever I felt sick. I loved that. I could fall asleep. It was next best to being home.

. . . I found a snake one day and decided to stuff it the way they do in museums, so I got all the proper equipment: scissors, a bucket of water to keep things clean, some cotton for the stuffing, and a needle and thread to sew it up. I became discouraged after his innards were all floating around in the bucket, and I figured he'd never look too good anyway, since his head had been run over to begin with, so I gave up and ripped a dead gopher apart with the neighbor boy. He took the head and I took the tail and we pulled. I did it to show how tough I could be, and to make my sister sick. She got sick and we put the gopher remains in a paper bag and left it behind the house.

. . . We moved. ✺

Subject Writing

"After the match the boy hugged our wrestler as if he were saying 'Thanks,' and then walked away with his crutches." —Mary Leahy

Description of a Person

The best descriptions are written from a position of authority. In other words, to create an effective description, a writer must either know the person well or take time to closely observe the subject. One important part of the total person is usually highlighted in a description.

One of a Kind

Discussion: Describe a person (or an animal) who has impressed you. Try to focus on one or two specific parts of the total person. Think in terms of physical features, personality traits, and/or mannerisms (gestures, laughter, etc.). Or think of the person's choice of clothing, music, or favorite pastime. Then decide how you will develop your writing. Will you share a story about this person? Will you provide a detailed look at the person's wildest outfit or strangest mannerism? Or will you more generally highlight some of your subject's strengths and/or weaknesses? Make sure that your writing includes plenty of details. Provided below are guidelines to help you develop your writing. Also read the model descriptions that follow.

Searching and Selecting

1. **Selecting** • Select a subject that is important to you and/or interests you. (If possible, let the person know that he or she will be the subject of your description. And by all means, use good judgment in the way you describe your subject.)

2. **Searching** • If you're unsure about a subject, see "Possible Topics" in the "Writing About a Person" section in your handbook. (Think of individuals you know that fit topics listed there.)

   Special Note: If you already know what you want to say about your subject, go right to your first draft. Otherwise, follow the guidelines under "Generating the Text."

Generating the Text

3. **Recording** • Review the suggestions in "Writing About a Person" for ideas on gathering details about a person. Try clustering ideas for your description. (Clustering will also help you identify a focus or main idea for your writing.)

4. **Reviewing** • Consider all your ideas and decide how you want to approach your description. (See "Discussion" above for ideas.) Plan accordingly.

Writing and Revising

5. **Writing** • If you're ready to write your first draft, go to work, putting in details wherever they fit. If you're not sure where to start, choose one or two key details and free-write.

6. **Revising** • Carefully review your first draft. Also ask a classmate to read your paper and explain to you how he or she pictures your subject based on your writing. Continue working with your description using your own thoughts and your classmate's remarks as a guide.

Evaluating

Does the writing form a meaningful whole, moving clearly and smoothly from the opening idea to the closing thought?

Do the details in the writing present the subject in an effective way?

Will readers find the treatment of the subject interesting?

Student Model

In the following description, student writer Chad Hockerman shares an entertaining look at one of his family's dogs. Note the humorous and playful tone maintained throughout the writing.

The opening description focuses on Benson's charming qualities.

The closing idea effectively summarizes Benson's role in the family.

Sit Yourself Down, Benson

Benson, our uninhibited and enthusiastic Yorkshire terrier, joined our family on my sister's fifteenth birthday, and he quickly charmed his way into our hearts and lives. Feisty, he sometimes gets into trouble, but he always makes us smile.

Because he is observant and intelligent, Benson learns quickly. Often, he learns too quickly! One day when I was eating a late lunch, I set Benson on a chair beside me at the kitchen table. Though he was only a few months old at the time, this apparently made a big impression on him. Ever since that first shared lunch, Benson tries to join us at the table for every occasion. As soon as anyone approaches the table to eat, work, study, or make cookies, his head pops up over the table's edge. This funny, chair-hopping habit has embarrassed my parents more than once as Benson has "met" insurance agents at the kitchen table, and "dined" with New Year's Eve guests at the dining room table. Now Benson is pursuing this talent one step further. He sits in on our piano lessons (on the piano bench), much to the teacher's surprise and amusement.

Always in the center of things, Benson is a devoted friend to Baxter, our older Yorkie; a nightly foot-warmer for my dad; an entertaining daily companion for my mom; and the best playmate we three kids have ever had. ✐

Student Model

In this model, student writer Mary Leahy describes an individual she doesn't know personally. She will, however, never forget this person. Read the description and learn why.

Courage

I have been a wrestling cheerleader for the past two years. I had a lot of fun going to all the meets and invitationals, but there is one experience that I will never forget.

We were wrestling many teams at an invitational and one of them was Beloit Turner. We were just about to begin when the 98 pounder from Turner came out on the mat, and I was in total shock. He was a small boy who had a lot of shoulder muscle but a very small waist and small legs. As he went out to the mat, the other cheerleaders and I noticed that he could barely walk without his crutches because he had some kind of leg defect. So he had to pull himself onto the mat. All of us cheerleaders were in awe. We couldn't believe this boy was going to wrestle.

Soon the match began, and the boy from Turner fell to his knees. He had to wrestle on his knees because he could not use his legs. Our wrestler took him down and finally won the match. After the match the boy hugged our wrestler as if he were saying "Thanks," and then walked away with his crutches.

This year when we wrestled Turner, that same boy was on the team. He was still wrestling even though he had lost almost every match.

To me, this boy had as much courage as anyone can have. Every time he went out on the mat to wrestle, he knew he wouldn't win; but he still tried and did his best! ✍

The subject is described according to his appearance and actions.

The writer concludes that this wrestler "had as much courage as anyone can have."

Student Model

We all have had close encounters with people less fortunate than ourselves. In the following model, learn about student writer Ben Westley's encounter with a homeless old man in a bus station. (This article first appeared in the April 1992 issue of *High School Writer*. It is reprinted with permission.)

The Old Blues Man

The first sentences introduce the subject and establish the setting of the description.

In the Pittsburgh bus station on a cold January night I saw a man who had a poignant, not so pleasant smell. This man looked as if he was in his late seventies, and he was dressed in an old, soiled, light blue suit with a pair of dull brown, patent leather shoes and a new tan winter coat that looked as if it had been given to him by a church or charity organization. Immediately, I realized this man was homeless.

I couldn't help but notice the disgusted looks on people's faces. I know he had to notice also. The old man showed no feeling towards the people's looks; it was as if he had learned to ignore them. He had seen so many of these repulsive looks that they just didn't affect him any longer. The security guards had been watching him and checked to see if he was drinking. I took it that he had not been because the guards left him alone.

The old man got up from his seat to talk to a man in an army uniform. He mentioned that he was in W.W. II. The man's only response was to yell, "Get outta my face, old man!"

One particular incident involving the older man is described in great detail.

The old man replied as he returned to his seat, "You've no respect, no respect at all." The old man began to hum an unfamiliar song. Slowly the words came stirring out of his mouth. He was singing the blues! I've heard blues songs before, but none seemed to mean anything until this old man sang them. The songs meant something to him. They seemed to be the story of his life. The man was immediately thrown out into the cold street by the security guards.

The sudden outburst of the blues had been brought on by the man in the army uniform because of his lack of caring, compassion, and, as the old man noticed, respect. If the man in the army uniform had just listened, maybe the old man would've had a warm place to sleep that night.

In closing, the writer reflects on this one-time encounter.

When my bus was making its departure, I noticed the homeless man. He looked at me and waved. Even though I hadn't said a word to him, I could tell that he probably appreciated the fact that I gave him common courtesy, by not making faces or running away from him. I'm glad he noticed; it made me proud. I only wish that I had talked to him. I'm sure I missed out on a few great stories and the chance to gain some insight into this life I encountered so briefly. ✑

Professional Model

In this model description of a person, the author provides an insightful and entertaining look at the most beautiful girl in his class in school. It is clear from this passage that Rivers Applewhite holds a very special place in the author's boyhood heart. (This excerpt from *Good Old Boy* by Willie Morris is reprinted with permission from Yoknapatawpha Press, Oxford, Mississippi.)

Good Old Boy

The writer immediately establishes Rivers' special place among his schooltime favorites.

This list of my schooltime favorites, Bubba, Spit, and all the rest, would not be complete without the one I think of the most: Rivers. Rivers Applewhite. She was without doubt the most beautiful girl in our class, but she was not a demure kind of beauty. Not at all. She wore her dark brown hair short (sometimes the way the models did in *Harper's Bazaar*) to offset her fine willowy grace, and she had deep green eyes, and in spring and summer she was always brown as a berry from all the time she spent in the sun. I am also pleased to say that she was not a tomboy; who in his proper senses would want a girl to kick a football farther than he could, or outrun him in the 50-yard dash?

The main part of the description contains specific details about Rivers' character and actions.

She was smart as could be—much smarter than Edith Stillwater, even though Edith got better grades—and she got Spit McGee through final exams in the third grade by bribing him, with the lemon pies she always was baking, to practice his long division and memorize poems. (Spit McGee once recited Browning: "Oh to be in April, Now that England's here.") She was also partial to Old Skip, my dog, and would bring him bones and cotton candy, so Skip was a regular old fool over Rivers Applewhite, sidling up to her with his tail wagging, putting his wet black nose against the palm of her hand, jumping and gyrating in her presence like the craziest creature alive.

In the closing points, the author reaffirms Rivers' special status.

Unlike some of the other girls, especially Edith Stillwater, she would never so much as consider telling the teacher on anybody, and to this day I cannot recall a traitorous or deceitful act on her part. Kind, beautiful, a fount of good fun and cheer, she was the best of all feminine symbols to the wild and unregenerate boys of Yazoo. All of us, dogs and boys alike, were a little bit in love with Rivers Applewhite. . . . ✐

Secondhand Story

In secondhand stories, writers share the stories and experiences of people around them. In planning these stories, writers must learn as much as they can about their subjects. This may require more than one conversation or sharing session with the people involved.

"Have I ever told you the story . . . ?"

Discussion: Share a memorable or noteworthy story told to you by someone you know well—a parent, grandparent, neighbor, or friend. This story should focus on a person's childhood, school years, or early adulthood; and it should give you new insight into the individual who shares the experience. Your main goal is to retell the story clearly and completely in as much detail as possible. Include background information and your own thoughts and feelings to go along with the story if necessary. Provided below are basic guidelines to help you develop your writing. Also note the sample stories following these guidelines.

Searching and Selecting

1. **Reviewing** • Think of unforgettable stories told to you by family members, neighbors, or friends. Try to recall what it was about these stories that made them interesting or exciting.

2. **Collecting** • If no writing ideas come readily to mind, gather a few stories by asking one or two people to share some of their most memorable experiences. Provide prompts to help people remember: "What do you remember most about school?" or "What made you feel the most proud?" You'll be rewarded with some great material if you only go out and find it. (Take notes as these stories are told, and, if at all possible, record them as well.)

Generating the Text

3. **Assessing** • Make sure that you understand all of the important details related to the story. If some parts seem unclear, ask the storyteller to explain or expand upon them.

4. **Focusing** • Try to figure out what it is that makes the story work for you, and let that be what stands out in your writing. Is it the sense of adventure? the humor? the pride? the sorrow? Also decide how you want to present your story. (Refer to the models for ideas.)

Writing and Revising

5. **Writing** • Write your first draft freely, working in details as they come to mind—or according to your planning.

6. **Revising** • Carefully review your first draft, and revise and refine as necessary. (Try reading it aloud to get a sense of the story's rhythm. Also ask a classmate to review your work.)

Evaluating

Is the writing focused around a specific experience, time, or story?

Does the writing contain effective detail, and does it move smoothly from beginning to end?

Will readers appreciate the treatment of the story?

Help File: Share a memorable story about someone from the present or the past that you've read about in a book, magazine, or newspaper.

Student Model

In the following story, student writer Carlos Lavezzari recounts the sudden and tragic death of his good friend. He begins by describing the scene outside his apartment building and then fills in all of the details as they were told to him secondhand. Note that this is a very immediate story, not what you would typically expect in this type of writing. (This story first appeared in the May 1992 issue of *New Youth Connections: The Magazine Written By and For New York Youth*. It is reprinted with permission.)

The writer sets the scene by describing the frantic state of affairs as he experienced them.

The writer shifts between his own observations and the story of the shooting as it was told to him.

In closing, the writer tries to come to terms with the tragic experience.

Remembering Mike

It was the winter of 1990, very close to Christmas. I remember coming home from a friend's house about 3:30 in the afternoon and seeing two Channel 7 news vans parked in front of my building. There were people all over the place in a frantic state. Some of my friends and neighbors were standing around, crying. I ran up to try to get someone to tell me what had happened. No one answered me so I went inside. In the lobby all of the holiday decorations were ripped down and the Christmas tree looked as if it had been trampled. Just then one of my friends came downstairs saying that Mike had been shot. I couldn't believe it. I had just played basketball with Mike the day before, and he was saying how one day he was going to play for the NBA. And now he was dead? I ran outside to see if it was true. I saw Mike's sister with a bewildered look on her face. One of my friends walked up to me and told me the first of many stories I was to hear about what had happened. He said Mike had been in a schoolyard with a Puerto Rican girl whose brother was the local gang's leader. Mike was sitting with the girl, eating. Three members of the gang walked up and told them that they were going to tell her brother.

I Never Said Thank You

When the girl's brother got there he said, "I don't want my sister 'round no n _ _ gers," and shot at everyone in the park. He caught one of my friends in the leg, another in the arm, and Mike in the chest. After hearing this I found myself wishing I had been there, thinking maybe I could have done something. Maybe I could have talked him into going home or been able to warn him about the type of person the girl's brother was. I started feeling bad, bad about the fact that I never told him how thankful I was for all the times he had my back in a fight, or for letting me hide in his house at times when people wanted to jump me. I never got to thank him for sneaking me into his house when I ran away from home, or for being a good friend to talk to when I was feeling down. The last thing I remember saying to him was, "See you tomorrow". . . ✍

Student Model

In "Rainy Day Memories," student writer Elizabeth Balin presents a wonderful story about her grandmother's childhood in Chicago. Note how this piece is really a story within a story. One story deals with the writer's restlessness; the other story deals with the grandmother's memories.

Rainy Day Memories

The rain came down in torrents outside, and I was trapped indoors. Brimming with the energy of youth, I had grown weary of coloring books, bored by the television, and bothered by the radio; now I wandered restlessly throughout the house in search of companionship.

Grandma Bea sat at the kitchen table with a steaming cup of coffee in her hand. She was staring out the nearby window at the grey sullen day, but one look at her faraway gaze told me that she was dreaming of lands far more distant than our backyard. Relieved to finally find the perfect audience, I flopped down beside her and put on my most practiced expression for pity.

"There's nothing to *do* around here," I whined.

She turned to me. My grandmother was eighty-six years old, and she was beautiful. Her wrinkled skin was an intricate map of wisdom and hard times, but the never-ending blue of her eyes hinted at eternal youth and vibrance. In a soothing expression of tenderness, she placed her gnarled hand upon mine and squeezed it gently.

"Have I ever told you the story?" she inquired.

I shook my head and signaled for her to continue.

"Why, when I was a little girl," she began, "there was always plenty to do . . ."

I watched, entranced, as she reached into the stores of her mind for the details. As she strained to remember, the room swirled with the shadows of rich experiences, the haze of lost loves, and the clouds of a mind that brimmed with nearly a century of memories.

"Oh yes. Now I remember. The year was 1919. . . ."

When the fog finally cleared, I saw sitting before me a young girl, about twelve years old, with flowing blonde curls. Her plump hand gripping mine, she was eagerly explaining her day.

In 1919, my grandmother was an extremely busy little girl. She was a part of a very large Jewish family of twelve that lived along Division Street in downtown Chicago. Today, most kids would complain about the burdens of sharing everything with six brothers and four sisters; to Beatrice, being part of a large family was the best gift that any child could ask for.

Her mother was a Hungarian Jew who packed her bags at age fourteen and left for America when she was refused schooling in Hungary. That incident probably explained her character; she was a strong-willed and determined lady who preached to her children to follow their dreams no matter how distant they might seem. With that in mind, it was no surprise that when her eldest son, Benjamin, returned from World War I with visions of movie theaters in his mind, she eagerly hocked her diamond earrings to pay for the venture. So began Chicago's Harmony Theaters.

Everyone in the family took a share of the work. One brother stood outside the theater, megaphone in hand, to advertise the latest features, while

---

The narrator's boredom sets the scene for the secondhand story to follow.

A magical sense of going back in time is suggested as the grandmother's story unfolds.

Specific details about work and play are provided throughout this story.

his younger sister prepared the projector for use. Benjamin would select the music rolls for the player organ that would accompany the silent movies, while Bea would wander through the movie house to collect the tickets.

"Do you remember any of the movies?" I interrupted.

"Of course! *A Child for Sale* was my favorite." She continued with her memories. It seems that for this flick, the child geniuses behind the Harmony Theaters put their creativity together and came up with a master plan. Poor Bea, only twelve years old, was dressed from head to toe in women's garb, high heeled shoes, and all the proper padding. She was handed a doll and buggy and was forced to walk the crowded streets of Chicago while her brothers passed out flyers behind her.

Bea's family also owned the Harmony Bakery, and ran it in much the same manner. Each morning, Bea woke up at five to hitch the delivery horses up and deliver the fresh-baked rolls and breads. Then it was off to grammar school. Come lunch hour, she would return to the bakery and work behind the counter to help sell their delectable pound cakes and sponge cakes to the local Americans, Germans, Jews, and Poles. With a smile on her lips, she'd hand them their wrapped packages and one small card that read:

"Harmony: Eat our bread, see our movies, and be happy."

"What was your fondest memory at the bakery?" I prodded.

Bea looked at me with a mischievous glimmer in her eye. "They had to stack the bread boxes up behind the counter so that I could reach the register." We laughed together.

On the infrequent occasions when the family had a break from all the work (barring Sabbath Sunday, of course), they would hitch the carriage to the delivery horses and take in the sights of Lincoln Park. Or they would all gather before the family fireplace and spend hours laughing and showing off their talents. Bessie would read Shakespeare and Ester would dance, Benjamin played a few tunes on the piano, and Bea, ever the extrovert, would display her fine elocution talents that she was sharpening at the local dramatic arts school.

"You wanted to be an actress?" I demanded with disbelief.

"Why not? I lived in the heart of a huge city of opportunity. Like my Mama always said, I deserved a share just as much as everyone else."

But my hasty interruption broke the story; the haze welled up, engulfed us, and then slowly cleared. My grandmother, ancient and withered, had returned, still squeezing my hand gently. She turned once again to peer at the dreary sky. As she gazed out, she mumbled something, so lightly that I strained forward to hear.

"Anything is possible if you just have the imagination to try."

With renewed vigor, I jumped up, gave dear Grandma the largest hug her fragile frame could endure, and ran away in search of my coat and galoshes. I left Grandma staring quietly out the window, already caught up in a new stream of memories. There would be other rainy days for her to share her wisdom with me.

As I turned my back to leave, I could have sworn that I saw a flash of golden curls. ✍

The writer asks her grandmother for more information—suggesting her sincere interest in Bea's story.

The writing comes to an effective close when the spell is broken and Bea and the writer return to their present-day worlds.

Professional Model

In the following secondhand story, you'll learn about one man's unforgettable experience during World War II. While the writers of the preceding models were close to their subjects, the writer of "Unforgettable" is a more objective journalist. His story is based on information he gathered during an interview session. ("Unforgettable" appeared in the July 6, 1992, issue of the *Milwaukee Journal* and is reprinted with permission by the Associated Press.)

The opening lines identify the incredible nature of this secondhand story.

The writer works in many of his subject's actual words.

The brief closing statement, "It was a dangerous job," provides a fitting closing.

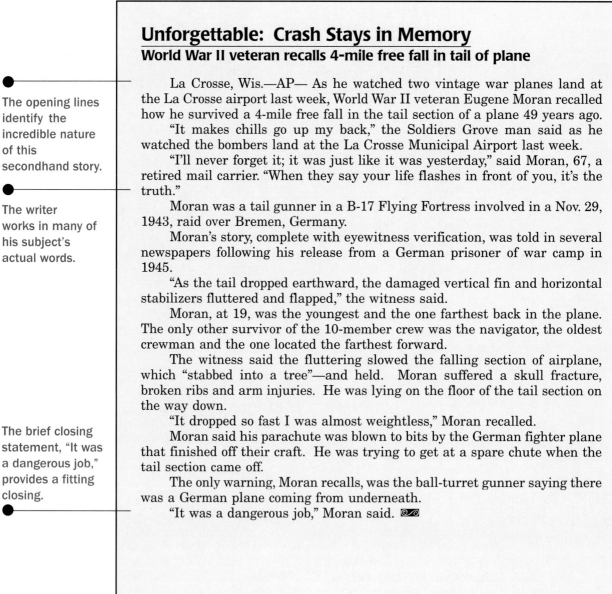

Unforgettable: Crash Stays in Memory
World War II veteran recalls 4-mile free fall in tail of plane

La Crosse, Wis.—AP— As he watched two vintage war planes land at the La Crosse airport last week, World War II veteran Eugene Moran recalled how he survived a 4-mile free fall in the tail section of a plane 49 years ago.

"It makes chills go up my back," the Soldiers Grove man said as he watched the bombers land at the La Crosse Municipal Airport last week.

"I'll never forget it; it was just like it was yesterday," said Moran, 67, a retired mail carrier. "When they say your life flashes in front of you, it's the truth."

Moran was a tail gunner in a B-17 Flying Fortress involved in a Nov. 29, 1943, raid over Bremen, Germany.

Moran's story, complete with eyewitness verification, was told in several newspapers following his release from a German prisoner of war camp in 1945.

"As the tail dropped earthward, the damaged vertical fin and horizontal stabilizers fluttered and flapped," the witness said.

Moran, at 19, was the youngest and the one farthest back in the plane. The only other survivor of the 10-member crew was the navigator, the oldest crewman and the one located the farthest forward.

The witness said the fluttering slowed the falling section of airplane, which "stabbed into a tree"—and held. Moran suffered a skull fracture, broken ribs and arm injuries. He was lying on the floor of the tail section on the way down.

"It dropped so fast I was almost weightless," Moran recalled.

Moran said his parachute was blown to bits by the German fighter plane that finished off their craft. He was trying to get at a spare chute when the tail section came off.

The only warning, Moran recalls, was the ball-turret gunner saying there was a German plane coming from underneath.

"It was a dangerous job," Moran said. ✑

"I was an eyewitness to a classic drug deal. The smoothness with which it was performed and the quickness of the transaction will be embedded in my mind forever." —Darren Johns

Eyewitness Account

In an eyewitness account, a writer shares the details of an event he or she has recently witnessed. The details are gathered through close observation— what was seen, heard, felt, and so on.

With My Own Eyes

Discussion: Recall the details of an event or incident you witnessed or observed. The subject of your writing should be an event that occurred in the **recent** past—something you witnessed within the past few weeks or so. How you develop your eyewitness account is up to you. You can report it as a news story, answering the 5 W's and H *(Who? What? Where? When? Why? and How?)* related to the event. You can compose a friendly letter, sharing the details of the event with a friend or family member. Or perhaps your account would be most effective as a journal entry, containing details related to the event plus your personal thoughts and feelings. Read the sample accounts that follow for ideas. Then refer to the guidelines below as you write.

Searching and Selecting

1. **Selecting** • If no event from your recent past comes to mind, keep your eyes open for possible subjects during a typical day. (You might, for example, focus on some action that regularly takes place in the school cafeteria.) You could attend a game, meeting, or concert. Be on the alert for surprising incidents to write about. Discuss writing ideas with your classmates.

   Special Note: At this point you can go right to your first draft. Or you can collect details and make some basic planning decisions by following the guidelines under "Generating the Text."

Generating the Text

2. **Collecting** • List as many details as you can about your subject. An eyewitness account is not just what you see. So, record the event using all your senses.

3. **Reviewing** • Review your notes to make sure you have recorded all of the important details. If you can remember any bits of dialogue (conversation), make sure to record them.

4. **Focusing** • Write a focus sentence identifying the most important idea or the main feelings you want to share with your readers related to the event. Decide which facts and details that you have collected will support this focus. Also consider what form your writing will take.

Writing and Revising

5. **Writing** • Write your first draft as thoughts and details related to the event come to mind— or according to your planning and organizing.

6. **Refining** • Read your first draft a number of times. As you read, ask yourself if you have included all of the important information and if you have arranged it in the best order. Revise and refine your writing accordingly.

Evaluating

Does the writing move smoothly and clearly from the opening ideas to the closing thoughts?

Does the writing contain enough specific detail?

Will readers appreciate the treatment of this event?

Student Model

In the following eyewitness account, student writer Darren Johns describes a drug deal he saw take place while he was at work one night. The strength of this account is its straightforward style. The drug deal, as it unfolded, is simply and honestly reported.

Drug Deal

I was an eyewitness to a classic drug deal. The smoothness with which it was performed and the quickness of the transaction will be embedded in my mind forever.

I was busy at work when I happened to observe the incident. My work place opens onto an alley behind the adjacent stores. Approximately 25 feet from the rear of the store is a dumpster. I had a moment of rest and glanced out the back door. When I looked, I saw a man in nice brand-name clothes come from the left and a raggedy-looking man come from the right. They both met by the dumpster in clear view from where I was standing. They both looked around, ignoring the door I was looking through, looking instead for anyone coming. They quickly exchanged packages and looked over what they received. The nicely dressed man flipped through the roll of bills he received and nodded. The raggedy man felt through and checked his package then gave a quick, assenting nod. Both men slipped their packages into their pockets and after a few quick glances, each went the way he had come. The whole incident took a maximum of 45 seconds.

The reason I will remember this incident is the rapidity of the exchange and its extreme likeness to the typical movie drug deal. It opened my eyes to how available drugs are "in my own backyard." It surprised me to see such a thing take place behind my own workplace. ✐

The opening line clearly sets the scene.

Only the most important details are provided. All the description centers around the two men and their exchange.

Student Model

In the following eyewitness account, student writer Ron St. Germain describes the night fire destroyed a neighbor's house. Note how powerful verbs and sensory details effectively re-create the scene for the readers. ("One Hot Night" appeared in *Kaleidoscope* [Amesbury Middle School], 1991.)

One Hot Night

Darkness fell over the gathering crowd and all was silent. A dim red spark shot into the air followed by millions of giant fiery flowers of pinks, golds, and silvers. Babies could be heard crying frantically. I sat watching in the field as the smell of gunpowder blew through the air. The show ended and I walked home in the steamy summer night.

I got in the door before my sister and dashed up the stairs. I grabbed a pair of shorts and hurled myself into the bathroom. The cold water from the faucet cooled my sweaty head. I went into my tiny room and slept as my wet hair drenched the soft pillow.

It was three o'clock when my mother came screaming into the hall waking us up. She told us to grab the dog and to get out of the house for safety. As I ran down the stairs, the temperature rose and as I opened the side door, I was hit with a blast of hot air like from an oven, with the sound of bottle rockets and exploding glass piercing my ears. I saw my neighbor's sleek red motorcycle pop and shrapnel shoot in all directions as the bright blaze engulfed the once shiny and beautiful Honda.

My family gathered in the front yard and watched with our neighbors as the house across the street went up in flames. No one spoke as the fire trucks came up the hill with lights flashing but no sirens on. The firefighters got the hoses attached together faster than lightning, but couldn't get any water pressure. The fire spread through the old house as the flames melted the black Toyota's brakes. It came rolling at our house with flames billowing from the windows, hood, and muffler. Luckily, it stopped as the rear wheel hit a fire hose.

Minutes later the water pressure from another hydrant was high and the flames started to die. More people gathered in horror as the smoke flew to the edge of the sky and made my eyes tear. It was getting hard to breathe and I was getting burned by the ashes as they flew by. As morning approached, two other cars parked in the charred garage slowly melted. The sun rose but no one could see it because of the thick screen of ash and smoke.

My friends and I sat and watched on the lawn as the last of the flames were extinguished. The firefighters then grabbed axes and charged in the house cutting holes in the roof. They threw out mattresses and clothing that were smoldering. They found a guitar case and brought it down. A minute later, down came the black filmed keys to the case. We all gathered around as the firefighter unlocked it. There lay a metallic blue guitar with only some water damage. They also found a jar of jewelry cleaner with a diamond ring at the bottom of the pink liquid.

I got mad at the people who walked or drove slowly by and stared at the house as the owners sat crying, wearing their only possessions.

After a few hours of sleep my friends and I took up a collection for our three homeless neighbors. That night, I wrapped the two hundred twenty-three dollars to present to them the next day.

The use of the first person "I" throughout the essay creates a sense of drama and urgency.

The event is recalled in great detail from the opening idea to the closing sentence.

Notice that the writing is organized around the writer's actions before, during, and after the fire.

Professional Model

In this eyewitness account, professional writer Robert Fulghum tells of a lovers' ritual at the Feast of St. John, a traditional ceremony held every summer in the south of France. Though eyewitness accounts can often be very straightforward—a recounting of the basic facts—they can also be written with a personal slant or around a dominant image. Like any good observer, Fulghum reports what he sees; but notice how he structures his observations around the image of the fire. By writing this way, he re-creates for the reader the mystery of the events he witnessed. (From *It Was on Fire When I Lay Down on It* by Robert Fulghum. Copyright © 1988, 1989 by Robert Fulghum. Reprinted by permission of Villard Books, a division of Random House, Inc.)

It Was on Fire When I Lay Down on It

The author identifies the time and place of action before jumping into his detailed account.

ONCE ON A MIDSUMMER'S EVE, in the farming village of Puyricard, near Aix-en-Provence in the south of France, my wife and I were taken to a celebration of the Feast of Saint John. (Which Saint John I do not know. There are many. If he provided a reason to celebrate with music and dance, then good on him, whoever he was.)

When the first star could be seen in the night sky, the villagers lit a bonfire in the dirty playfield of the school, and a folk band began to play—guitar, bass drum, shepherd's flute and concertina. Music that was close at hand and long ago at the same time. In a universal two-step, couples danced, encircling the great fire—their only light. Lovely. A scene from a novel, a film, a hopeful imagination.

The writer reports what he sees—the first lovers jumping over the fire—before he explains the ritual. This helps capture the excitement of the moment.

At the first intermission, the couples did not leave for refreshment, but stood staring into the bonfire. Suddenly an athletic young man and woman, holding each other tightly by the hand, ran and leaped high in the air through the fierce flames, landing safely just beyond the edge of the coals. As the crowd applauded, the two embraced and walked away, wearing expressions of fearful joy, having tempted the fates and emerged unscathed to dance once more. Make no mistake about it, what they had done was quite dangerous.

And it was this leaping through the fire that was at the heart of the Feast of Saint John.

It worked this way: If you were lovers, married or not, or if you were just friends, even, and you wanted to seal your covenant, you made a wish together that you would never part, and then you rushed the fire and jumped over while holding hands. It was said that the hotter the fire and the higher the flames, the longer and closer would be the companionship. But it was also said that if you misjudged the fire and got singed or came down in the coals on the other side or lost your grip on one another while jumping, then evil would come to you and your bond. Not to be taken lightly, this.

In closing, the writer explains the importance of his account.

So the young of heart and fleet of foot jumped early on; as the evening grew darker and the fire burned lower, the more cautious made their moves. Some did not clear the fire; some jumped too soon and some too late and some ran to the fire only to stop short, and some broke their grip, with one partner jumping while the other held back at the last moment.

Though there was much laughter and cheering and teasing, it was also very clear that this was ancient and serious business. Not just another party. Once a year, late in the night of high summer, with music and dance to lift the spirit, you took your love by the hand and tempted the fire of destiny. . . . ☯

"Mass whale suicides, or 'strandings' as they are called, occur year after year with disturbing consistency." —from "Suicide by Stranding"

Summary Report from Single Source

In preparing a summary from a single source, a writer selects an interesting article or chapter to read and analyze. The results of this careful reading are presented in a brief report that highlights the main points in the article.

"Good things, when short, are twice as good."

Discussion: Find an interesting, two- or three-page article in a recent *Time*, *Newsweek*, or *U.S. News & World Report*. Read it carefully. Then ask three questions: (1) What is the main idea or point of the article? (2) What information (statistics, surveys, examples, etc.) does the author use to support the point? and (3) How does the information make the point seem true or believable? Then write a summary—a shortened version of the article—by working through the steps below. Also note the model summaries that follow. (For more help, see "Summary, writing the" in the index of your handbook.)

Searching and Selecting

1. **Reviewing** • Glance through several magazines, looking at titles of articles, pictures, graphs, etc. Skim articles that seem interesting and fit the assignment.

2. **Selecting** • From these articles, pick the one that (a) is most interesting, (b) makes the best point, and (c) supports the point with believable information.

Generating the Text

3. **Noting** • Work through the article, looking for the key ideas and most important information. List those ideas on a piece of paper. Also, list basic details that tell the *who*, *what*, *when*, *where*, and *why* of the story.

4. **Assessing** • Review your article and your notes. Does the list include the key ideas? Does it include information needed to support the ideas? Do you fully understand the point and importance of the article?

5. **Focusing** • Skim the article once more. Then skim your notes again. Do you feel ready to tell a friend what this article is about? What information must your friend know? What do you want to say first? Next? Last? Organize your ideas in an outline or some other form.

Writing and Revising

6. **Writing** • Write the first draft of your report as if you were telling your friend about the article. Remember your friend needs to understand (a) the author's main point, (b) the author's key supporting ideas, and (c) the information the author uses to make his/her article important and believable.

7. **Revising** • Review, revise, and refine your paper. Is the summary fair—does it stick to what the author said? Is it complete—does it include all of the important information? Is your writing clear—will your friend understand? Share your paper with others and revise accordingly.

Evaluating

Does the summary show an understanding of what the author is saying?

Is the summary fair, clear, and complete?

Is the article reduced to an appropriate "summary" length?

Student Model

In this report, the writer presents a clear, accurate, and understandable summary of whale strandings. Because the complex topic is explained clearly and concisely, readers gain insight into a phenomenon that has puzzled people for centuries.

The opening lines set the scene and introduce the subject.

"Strandings" are defined, and the writer accurately summarizes the history of this phenomenon.

The final paragraph ties all of the theories together and makes a clear summary statement.

Suicide by Stranding

Picture a New England beach in autumn. The sky is clear, the sun warms your face, competing with the cool breeze, and the green sea has washed ashore almost 100 of its most magnificent creatures to die. A biologist walks among the bloating bodies of the whales, and he is clearly puzzled.

Mass whale suicides, or "strandings" as they are called, occur year after year with disturbing consistency. Many men have tried to understand these bizarre suicides. Even Aristotle, the ancient Greek philosopher, thought about the whales' deaths. Although he decided the suicides may indeed happen "without any apparent reason," modern biologists are not so easily convinced.

One researcher pointed out that the whales are descended from land-dwelling animals. He decided the whales may simply be "remembering" their ancient roots and beaching themselves to "go home." This habit, however, would have put the whales close to extinction years ago. The idea had to be dismissed.

A newer theory suggests that the whales blindly follow their food supplies into shallow water. For example, they may swim after a shoal of squid, quickly eat their dinner, and then find themselves too close to shore for comfort.

Another theory says that whales follow the earth's magnetic forces. As though they were following a road map, the whales travel wherever these forces lead. Unfortunately, the magnetic flow will sometimes intersect the shore and guide the whales along a collision course with the beach.

Biologists realize, of course, that none of these findings are complete explanations. They feel that the strandings must have a number of causes, not just one. To make this point, they compare beached whales to crashed planes. One theory will never explain them all. ✍

Professional Model

Summary reports in magazines and newspapers provide an invaluable service to the reading public by providing scaled-down versions of complex stories. In the following professional model, writer Steven Findlay provides an alarming report related to AIDS research. (This report first appeared in the August 3, 1992, issue of *U.S. News & World Report.* Copyright 1992, *U.S. News & World Report.* It is reprinted with permission.)

The main point of this summary report—a new virus causing an AIDS-like illness—is clearly identified in the first paragraph.

The facts and details related to this new finding are outlined in the second paragraph.

The Shock of the New

Again and again, AIDS has provided powerful lessons in how little is really known about the mysterious world of viruses. Scientists and AIDS activists—including protesters angry about the high cost of treatment and the low investment in research—who convened last week in Amsterdam for the Eighth International Conference on AIDS were reminded anew of their frustrating ignorance. The meeting was rocked by reports—not slated for its official agenda—of a possible new virus causing an AIDS-like illness. Health officials scurried to gather information, put the finding in context and calm public fears. There was no threat to the blood supply, they promised. And even if it was a new virus, it did not seem to be spreading rapidly or to be easily transmitted through sex. But by week's end, as some scientists sounded notes of urgency, the World Health Organization was planning a special meeting within the next month to probe the finding. "This problem will be very, very actively pursued," pledged Anthony Fauci, head of AIDS research at the U.S. National Institutes of Health.

What is known now is this: Between 24 and 30 people in the United States and Europe have developed the AIDS-like illness, but their blood has shown no signs of HIV, the virus that causes AIDS. Three separate teams of U.S. researchers say they have detected the presence of a new virus, or found viral particles, in the blood of a dozen of these people. The teams were not claiming to have found the same virus, though, and other leading AIDS experts and virologists cautioned that complete testing has not been done to rule out known viruses. One explanation is that the researchers are seeing an AIDS-like disease caused by a rare virus—perhaps a mutated animal virus—that has been around for a long time but never previously identified. Another is that some or all of the people with the AIDS-like illness are infected with a mutant form of HIV not detectable with current blood tests. Indeed, other researchers reported at the meeting that a new and unusual strain of HIV appears to be spreading rapidly among heterosexuals in Thailand. For all the gains in understanding AIDS, scientists admitted at the conference's closing sessions that a vaccine, much less a cure, remains an elusive goal. ✐

Professional Model

Did you know Bambi isn't as innocent as you thought? Read this eye-opening summary report about the threat "Bambi and his deadly pals" present to unsuspecting motorists. Note writer Dan Bensimhon's entertaining and informative handling of a serious subject. (Reprinted by permission of *Men's Health Magazine*. Copyright 1992 [April] Rodale Press, Inc. All rights reserved.)

Man-Killers

You worry about grizzly bears and sharks.
We're keeping an eye peeled
for Bambi and his deadly pals.

Every year just about 200 Americans are killed in unfortunate encounters with various wild and domesticated animals. That's not a particularly large number—more people probably die in the average Steven Seagal movie—and it should come as no surprise, considering that this big wilderness of a country we live in harbors a virtual army of poisonous snakes, aggressive insects, vicious dogs, hungry sharks, and bears ticked off about Winnebago-driving campers polluting the woods.

What is rather shocking is that when the statistics are broken down, none of these fearsome beasts can compare to the mild-mannered deer. In many areas, the deer population has boomed while their territory has been increasingly crisscrossed by roads and highways. For some reason, deer have yet to recognize mammoth chunks of speeding metal with two blazing eyes as a potential threat, and most motorists fail to consider the possibility of a 150-pound animal wandering into their path until it actually appears in their headlight beams.

The result, according to the National Highway Traffic Safety Administration, was more than 130 deer-related fatalities in 1989 alone. (Nobody's keeping track of how many deer buy the farm in these accidents.) That's more than three times the carnage wrought by the next deadliest critter on our list of man-killers, itself no nightmare of drooling fangs and razor-sharp claws. Forget about lions and tigers and bears. Just keep a sharp eye out for Bambi, bees and man's best friend. ◙

Man-Killer	Deaths Caused Per Year*
1. Deer	131.
2. Bees	43.
3. Dogs	14.
4. Rattlesnakes	10.
5. Spiders	4.
6. Sharks	1.
7. Captive elephants	1.
8. Scorpions	.67
9. Rats	.33
10. Goats	.33
11. Captive leopards	.33
12. Jellyfish	.24
13. Coral snakes	.20
14. Alligators	.17
15. Grizzly bears	.13
16. Mountain lions	.11
17. Captive monkeys	.05
18. Stingrays	.05
19. Vultures	.01
20. Killer whales	.01

Figures lower than 1.0 are averages, based on the best available records or the estimates of experts in the field for a given multi-year period.

The report begins with a statement of a problem and then summarizes the conditions that contribute to it.

In the chart, fatalities involving other animals are compared to fatalities involving deer.

The writer reveals the source of his summary report and closes by identifying the top three causes of death by animals (or insects).

Creative Writing

"The thing is, I really like to listen to him go on because, mainly, I like him. But if he never wants to listen to me, after a while, I get this horrible lonely feeling." —Norma Fox Mazer

Fictionalized Journal Entry

In fictionalized journal entries, writers think and write as if they were other people, real or imagined. The key to writing effective entries is to make them sound like real people talking about important concerns or issues.

A Day in the Life of . . .

Discussion: Create one or more journal entries as if they were written by an individual that you have read about, by an important figure currently in the news, by a person you have seen or know about, or by an imagined character completely of your own making. Your journal entries can focus on a significant event that has just taken place. They can discuss something soon to happen. Or, they can make general observations about daily living. Read the models that follow to get ideas for your writing; then refer to the guidelines below to help you develop your work.

Searching and Selecting

1. **Listing** • Write the following labels across the top of a piece of paper turned lengthwise: *musicians, history makers, adventurers, characters* (literature or movies), and *news makers*. List names of people under each category that you know about or are interested in. Create journal entries for one of these individuals.

2. **Selecting** • You may also consider people you know or have noticed on your way to and from school or work. Or, start with a specific event or situation (a Civil War battle, a gang war, a school in the future, etc.) and write about it from the point of view of an imagined character.

Generating the Text

3. **Collecting** • Get to know as much as you can about your subject. Imagine how he or she might carry on a conversation, and how he or she might react in different situations. Read about your subject if this person is noteworthy or newsworthy.

4. **Focusing** • To prepare for writing, ask yourself the following types of questions: What will my subject write about? What will be the tone of the writing (serious, informal)? How will the entries be structured? (See the models for ideas.)

Writing and Revising

5. **Writing** • Write the first draft of your entries according to your planning and organizing. Remember to write as if you are your subject. (See "Help File.")

6. **Revising** • Read your entries a number of times to make sure that you have captured the personality of your subject as you have imagined it. Revise and refine accordingly.

Evaluating

Are the basic elements (facts, language, etc.) consistent throughout the writing?

Has proper attention been given to accuracy for historical journals, or for journals dealing with real people and real events?

Will readers appreciate the way the character is presented?

Help File: Attach a brief explanation to your work, identifying who is speaking in the entries, what this person is writing about, why you selected this individual as the subject of your work, any sources of information you referred to, and so on.

Student Model

A fictionalized journal assignment presented student writer Heather Bachman with the perfect opportunity to explore a subject she found fascinating—the days of the mythical hero Robin Hood. What follows are four of her entries, written from the point of view of Maid Marian.

The first entry identifies the reason why Maid Marian is writing and provides some background information about her world.

Maid Marian

June 18, 1448

Today I had my 18th birthday. My father, Lord Locksley, presented me with an imported Arabian mare. Knowing how much I enjoy riding through Sherwood Forest, he thought that I should have my own horse. This leather-bound diary is a gift from my mother, Lady Locksley. To start off my entries, I should like to write about our castle and the life of nobility. Stone walls make the castle a fortress. Interior walls are polished wood. Pointed towers stand guard at each corner of the square castle. Surrounded by different rooms and chambers is the spacious courtyard. Stables for the horses are against the east wall of the castle. Stablehands live in the tackroom where they have cots to sleep on. Small paddocks hold our pigs, sheep, and goats. Geese, ducks, and chickens wander the stables and courtyard. Along the north wall are the kitchen and the great hall. Our cooks live in a room above the kitchen. We spend most of our time in the great hall. Many a minstrel has entertained our guests at a great feast in the great hall.

Since religion is an important part of our lives, a chapel is along the west wall. Although our priest is good and kind, I am suspicious of Nottingham's Bishop. Soldiers guard and live in the gatehouse in the south wall. Thanks to our guards, no unwelcome visitors ever get through. Just beyond the gatehouse are our rooms. My mother and father have a large room on the second floor. I live on the top floor. On clear nights I can gaze from my balcony and look at the stars. Large fireplaces keep us warm while candles and torches light the otherwise dark corridors.

It is getting dark and I must not waste candles.

Tomorrow I get to ride my new mare for the first time.

June 19, 1448

Today was wonderful and yet I cannot tell anyone but my diary. While riding through Sherwood Forest I met someone whom many nobles, including my own father, would like to see dead. Robin Hood. At first I thought he was going to attack and rob me, but he merely asked who I was and let me pass by. Perhaps tomorrow I shall see him again.

June 26, 1448

Unfortunately I haven't gotten to Sherwood Forest lately. We had the "honor" of having two of Nottingham's most esteemed individuals, the Sheriff and the Bishop, over for dinner. As we ate roasted pig, they discussed the state of politics and the Church. "More taxes must be placed on the peasants," claimed the Sheriff. Many peasants are in debt already, but the Sheriff doesn't care. He wants the riches he needs to continue his luxurious life. Even the Bishop feels that more taxes should be raised if the Church is expected to thrive. Basically that means that his chambers and his clothes will be more disgustingly lavish than they are already. How can the Church thrive if its members are penniless? Such corruption has poisoned our community.

But moral corruption isn't all that is poisoning our community. Black Death is what they call it. Peasants and nobles alike are falling victim to this terrible savage. My uncle, Lord Dulston, died just this morning. I overheard my father telling my mother about some peasants that the guards saw this morning. They said huge red swellings were on their necks. Others were lying in the paths by their houses writhing and coughing up blood! Even the animals aren't safe. Goats and sheep lie dead in the pastures. Fearing this scourge, my father allows no one new to enter the castle. Even future visits by the Sheriff have been cancelled for now (thank goodness)! I pray that God protect us from this silent killer.

July 5, 1448

Finally I got the chance to sneak a ride into Sherwood Forest. Robin was there. This time we began talking. I discovered he is 20 years old and leads a band of men who help him attain justice. His camp is deep in the dark eerie woods. While I warmed my hands near the fire, Robin explained his convictions. He robs the rich not for himself, but for the poor. Only a small amount of what they get is kept to support their cause. Peasants love Robin and his men, so no reward offered by the nobles does any good. I told him about the taxes the Sheriff and the Bishop are planning and Robin looked very upset. "Will it never end?" he sighed. "Soon the peasants will have nothing left." He fears that a revolt by the peasants may be their only way to retaliate. Hopefully it won't reach that extreme. As it was getting late Robin escorted me to the edge of the forest. Although my father looked doubtful when I said I'd fallen asleep under a tree near a brook, he didn't say anything. ✍

The writer presents matters of Church, State, and life as a teenager might see them.

It is clear from these entries that Ms. Bachman researched the myth of Robin Hood.

Student Model

For a history assignment, Heather Bachman writes a fictional journal entry as if she were making plans for a camel-caravan trip to Baghdad. It is obvious from her writing that Ms. Bachman has spent quite a bit of time researching her subject.

In the Days of the Caravans

Day one:

Today I went to the market to buy supplies for my trip to Baghdad (to trade).

Sheira, the butcher, sold me the pot of grease my servants and I will need for our lips. The hot desert winds are particularly bad this year, and the grease is the best way to prevent chapped lips.

There was a good crop of dates this year, so I bought thirty pounds of them very cheaply. Dates are very good and very filling, a good thing to have on a trip.

Olpim had many bags of dried rice that were full of plump, bright grains, well worth the price for fifty bags.

I was surprised to find that Bahir, the camel man, did not have the long, tender strips of dried camel meat. He had lost two camels in a sandstorm and so could not spare any for meat. Even though camel meat is tough, it is a good thing to have for food, so I had to slaughter one of my own yearling calves. Not only will I use the meat, but the fat in the hump can be used for butter. Its hide will be tanned and can be used for clothing, tents, shoes, water bags, pack saddles, and the fur will be woven by my wife into fine cloth that can be used for warm blankets and garments.

I was happy to discover that all five of my cows (female camels) are nursing babies. My wife will care for the babies while I am gone, and I will milk the camels every night for myself and the six servants in my caravan.

As usual, my friend Balika lent me his fine pack of Salukis, the best dogs for getting antelope or smaller game. The dogs will be fed a strip of camel meat every night. Balika also was nice enough to lend his falcon for my trip. The falcon can get the small game that the dogs might miss. In return for his kindness, I will bring him a leather water carrier from Baghdad. They have many leather workers in the markets there, and they have finely made water-tight carriers.

My wife spent all day filling the five huge goatskin water carriers. Although I have mapped out water holes where we can stop, the desert is too untrustworthy not to take water along. The five carriers carry enough water to let us survive quite a long time.

My wife also has spent the last two days collecting the camels' dung and letting it dry into "chips." These chips are a reliable fuel; and if we run out, it will be easy enough to get more from the camels in the caravan.

Although the heavy woven outfits my six servants and I must wear are uncomfortable, they are necessary to prevent sunburn and to slow evaporation.

Authentic names and unusual details immediately draw the reader into this journal entry.

Note how the caravan driver speaks in his journal just as he might in conversation with a friend.

The writer smoothly works interesting facts (like the "deadly mud traps") into her journal entries.

It has been very rainy this year, so I will have two servants walk ahead to look for the deadly mud traps. They are formed by heavy rains when the deceivingly dry crust hides deadly "snares."

The cool nights of the desert will be a welcome thing after spending all day in the hot sun.

Day two:

Supplies have all been packed tightly into sacks and are stacked in our tent, waiting to be loaded on the camels tomorrow. Balika's dogs are tied outside; they too wait for the trip to begin.

Trade materials were also packed today. This year I will be taking the following items to Baghdad: cloth for the nobles, paper for the printers, Arabian fillies, leather for the bookbinders and leather workers, and various pieces of jewelry.

My wife has been very busy weaving various cloths and making fine paper for trade. Today I packed the cloth and paper into five sacks that will be on one of my camels. My wife got the wool for her cloth from the small herd of ten ewes that she has. It sure takes a lot of work to shear the sheep and prepare the wool for weaving, but it is worth it. The two Arabian fillies she raised this year are black, a rare color, and that will make them very valuable. I will trade one for two camels. The other will be kept for breeding.

This year I will be taking new products to Baghdad. Pearls and some jewelry. I collected the pearls during trips to the gulf, and the jewelry my wife made from the dried, ivorylike bones of our camels. ⚉

Student Model

In the following entry, Oliver Garrison Terrell, an expert in the field of high-powered lasers, a man chosen to create a means of defeating the aliens, records his discoveries regarding an alien language. This journal entry is part of a short story entitled "Check and Checkmate" by Jon Leitheusser.

Date: December 30th, 1999

The description of specific details about the aliens' physical makeup lends realism to the writing.

I came upon something interesting today. I managed, this morning, to crack the aliens' language. Linguistics has always been an interest of mine, but I thought it might be impossible to understand this language. Everyone has been assuming that the language would be quite complex, because the aliens have two mouths; but late last night I heard from a colleague of mine, who is a doctor studying the corpses of the aliens, that the aliens have specialized mouths. The lower one is only for ingesting food and has an esophagus that leads to a digestive tract. Only the upper mouth is for speaking; they have a spoken language, like ours, that represents ideas and things with sounds. So while everyone else was puzzling away, trying to figure out how the two mouths worked in unison to create the language represented on the computer, I now had the key to working out the language on simpler terms, not having to worry about the presence of a second, speaking mouth—since there was none. I asked the man not to tell anyone else about this fact, wanting to beat everyone else to the end of the puzzle. It's become like a game to us. There are pools among us as to who will be the first to decipher the language.

The steps in the process used to decipher the aliens' language make the solution seem believable.

I stayed up all last night, excited about my secret knowledge, and continued working on the language. I have made more thorough notes in another booklet, so I don't have to look through here when I want to find something; but I have found that the language contains sounds that are most common. In this case, it is a low, squealing "f" sound (quite an interesting noise). I discovered that this sound is present in almost every word, and decided that it is the key to the language. Working on this assumption, I discovered that all sounds before the "f" sound are prefixes that modify the word that immediately follows the "f" sound. In other words, the word that follows the "f" sound is the root word, and everything that comes before it describes or modifies the root word. I then identified some of the most common prefixes and decided to do some work in the pod we have under study here.

At ten this morning, just after I finished deciphering the language, I went to the warehouse where the pod is kept. I was let in (I have full clearance still, even though my job is really over) and went to the pod. I asked if I could get inside, and that was all right. So, I climbed in and sat in the pilot's chair. I had the technicians close up the machinery and the door. When this had been done, the screen that now fully encompassed me lit up. This was the first I had seen this, but I had heard about it. The color is kind of . . . off. Not off-white, or off-brown, or off-grey, but . . . off. It's very hard to describe (obviously the aliens do not see only within our spectrum).

The writer's specific description of the advanced computer adds more realism to the journal entry.

The computers started scrolling words up the screens, some of which I could recognize, and then after a few minutes the scrolling stopped, and nothing happened. This was the point where we had always had to stop before, not knowing what to say or push. But I had understood a little and attempted to use the word I thought was the correct one. When I did, I felt a slight electrical charge run through me. I froze. I hoped I had not done anything wrong, but within the same second, the screens changed and started scrolling new information at me. Again I understood some, but most was lost to me. Along with the words on the screen came sound. The computer had a very advanced sound processor and spoke the words that flashed on the screen. The screen slowly faded the words away, but the voice kept speaking, until it revealed a perfect duplication of the immediate surroundings of the pod. Virtual reality. More advanced than anything we had. I could see everything outside the pod perfectly; the technicians leaning against their machines, the hangar doors, the crates in the corner . . . the mouse on the ground near the crates. It was incredible. And utterly real. I looked behind me and saw what would have been behind me had I been standing where the pod was. Amazing. This would revolutionize our virtual-reality technology.

Professional Model

In Norma Fox Mazer's short story "Up on Fong Mountain," Jessie has been assigned to write a series of journal entries about herself. Three of these entries are included here. ("Up on Fong Mountain," from *Dear Bill, Remember Me? and Other Stories* by Norma Fox Mazer. Copyright © 1976 by Norma Fox Mazer. Used by permission of Dell Books, a division of Bantam Doubleday Dell Publishing Group, Inc.)

A brief introduction predicts the subject of Jessie's journal.

Up on Fong Mountain

TO: All Students Taking English 10
MEMO FROM: Carol Durmacher
DATE: February 3
"That favorite subject, Myself."—James Boswell

Wednesday, March 26

Mom thinks she and I are alike. She's always saying it. (She thinks Dad and Anita are alike, she says they are both very good-looking. True. While she and I are both chunky and sandy-haired.) *But* Mom doesn't say boo to Dad, she's always very sweet to him. (Actually she's sort of sweet to everybody.) I'm not like her in that way *at all*. *I'm not sweet*. In that regard, I'm more like my father than Anita is. I became aware of this because of BD. I have been noticing that he likes things his own way. Most of the time he gets it. I have noticed, too, that I don't feel sweet about this at all!

March 29, Sat. afternoon

In addition to what she says about herself, Jessie's responses to other people reveal something about her personality.

BD came over last night and said we were going bowling. I said why didn't we do something else, as we went bowling last week. He said he liked bowling and what else was there to do, anyway? I said we could go roller skating. BD laughed a lot. I said what's the problem with roller skating. I like roller skating. (Which I do.) BD said, "Jessie, why are you being so picky? Why are you being so hard to get along with?" I thought, Right! Why am I?

And we went bowling. And then, later, I realized, just like that, he had talked me out of what I wanted to do and into what he wanted to do.

Monday, March 31, last day of the month

I don't even mind writing in here anymore, Miss Durmacher. I have plenty to write all the time. Now, lately, I've been thinking about what you wrote at the top of our assignment sheet. That favorite subject, Myself. Everyone got a laugh out of that when we first read it. Who wants to admit they are their own best, most favorite topic of conversation?

But I think it's the truth. Last night, at supper, Dad was talking, and I noticed how I was pretty much waiting to get my own two cents in. It seems Anita was, too, because she actually beat me to the punch. The only one who didn't rush to talk about herself was Mom, and sometimes I think that's just from long years of practice listening to Dad.

Also, today, I noticed when BD and I were hanging around school that he is another one whose most favorite subject is—myself. That is—*himself*. The thing is, I really like to listen to him go on because, mainly, I like him. But if he never wants to listen to me, after a while, I get this horrible lonely feeling. I think that's it. A lonely feeling. Sad. ✐

"The machinery, the furniture, the land were no longer his—but the farm and the home and the memories were his forever." —Lisa Servais

Character Sketch

In a character sketch, a writer brings an interesting character to life through a single action, event, conversation, or incident. An effective character sketch will reveal something important about the subject's personality, background, or beliefs.

I'd like you to meet someone.

Discussion: Create a character who reveals something important about his or her personality, background, or beliefs in a character sketch. A character sketch should read like a very, very short story dealing with one action, event, conversation, or incident. Try not to explain or describe too much about your character in your writing. Instead, let this person's own actions, words, and thoughts speak for themselves. Read the models that follow to learn more about writing character sketches. Also refer to the guidelines below to help you develop your writing.

Searching and Selecting

1. **Searching** • Fictional characters often display qualities of real people, so think of individuals you know or have heard about as a starting point for your subject search. Ask yourself which of their traits and mannerisms you might borrow for this activity. Remember, however, that you are creating a fictional character; your writing should not make any references to a real person.

2. **Selecting** • Or, start with a list of personal qualities (honesty, selfishness, stubbornness, etc.) and create characters who display these qualities. Also think of different situations (walking through a mall, riding in a bus, waiting for the principal, etc.). Whom could you put in one of these situations, and what would this character say or do?

Generating the Text

3. **Noting** • Form a picture of your character in your mind. What kind of clothes does this person like to wear? Does your character like to use jazzy street language or repeat "you know" about every fifth word? How does your character generally act or do things? What are this person's interests? In short, become well acquainted with your character.

4. **Focusing** • As your character comes alive in your mind, think of a specific setting or situation in which to place him or her. Remember: a character sketch is a mini-story dealing with a brief conversation, incident, meeting, event, etc.

Writing and Refining

5. **Writing** • Place your character right in the middle of a situation or an action and start writing from there. Let your character's words and actions speak for themselves as much as possible. Also work in a supporting character or two if necessary. Continue writing until your sketch comes to a natural stopping point or ending.

6. **Revising** • Read your draft carefully, paying special attention to the way your character is portrayed and the way your sketch moves along from one point to the next. Revise and refine accordingly.

Evaluating

?······?

Does the writing present a character in action?

Is the character effectively presented or portrayed?

Will readers appreciate the treatment of this subject?

Student Model

In this model, student writer Lisa Servais brings an elderly farmer to life. The sketch evolves around a specific incident, an auction at which the man and his wife watched their possessions being sold.

The mixture of physical and personal details allows readers to see the farmer and his wife inside and out.

The sketch unfolds through the all-knowing eyes of a narrator who lets readers know what the farmer is seeing and thinking.

Sold Out

The old man grumbled a bit as he wiped his eye with the back of his gnarled hand. From his perch above the crowd, he watched. He glanced at his wife standing a short distance away. She too was old, but still he saw in her wrinkled face the pretty girl he had asked to share his life. As he watched her, his thoughts began to wander. He thought about the white and blue dishes on which she had so proudly served him his first "home-cooked" meal. He seldom thought about such things, but at this moment they seemed very important to him. The chairs, the tables, the curtains, the things that had made the house seem more like a home—all somehow seemed very important to him.

He watched as his wife turned and looked at the seemingly ancient saddles and bridles hanging on the back of one of the wagons. He followed her eyes and found himself thinking about their first team of horses and how hard they had worked together. He remembered the time he had taken the team to the county fair horse pull, only to discover he didn't have the three-dollar fee needed to enter.

The auctioneer's voice droned on. He shifted in the seat of his old John Deere. He patted the sweat-worn leather seat. John Deere had been a fine friend; now it would plow someone else's field. The things he had worked for all his life were being auctioned away, piece by piece. He could do nothing but watch. A half century of life and feelings went with each piece. The machinery, the furniture, the land were no longer his—but the farm and the home and the memories were his forever. ✍

Student Model

Fictional characters, like real people, reveal a great deal about themselves by what they say and how they say it. Good writers often use dialogue in presenting and developing a character. The passage below by Jon Leitheusser, a student writer, illustrates just how effective dialogue can be.

Last Rites

All of the information about Cyril comes through his conversation with Al.

"You do realize that this meal is costing you an hour or so of work?" Al asked.

"Actually it's costing me the day. But so what? I'm a man working, not a working man. Work doesn't rule my life."

"Emerson. I'm impressed. You're college educated, huh?" Al asked.

"Yes and no. I went to college for a while, but I thought it was dumb," Cyril answered.

"Really? Why?"

Cyril's explanation of why he stopped going to college reveals an important character trait.

"Because I was sitting in the park reading one day and there was a group of people sitting a little ways away talking. I was tired of reading, so I sat there and listened to what they were talking about, and it hit me that they weren't talking about what they thought; they were talking about what a bunch of other people had said. And as I sat there listening, I realized that they were talking about these other people's beliefs as if they were their own. After a while I got up and walked away. I thought that maybe that was an isolated incident, so everywhere I went I started listening to what people around me were saying. And I found that no one at school seemed to be thinking for themselves. You know what I mean?"

"Yes. I think I know what you mean. You're pretty observant. So you dropped out of school," replied Al.

"Not right away. I waited another semester to see if things were going to change. They didn't, so I left. I figured that I could read and think and educate myself."

"Hmmm. Let me guess; you never got around to educating yourself and so you ended up working construction?"

"Nope. I still read as much as I can, but I need money to eat," Cyril said. "Right now I'm reading *Mythology* by Edith Hamilton. I like mythology. It's interesting to see how much it applies to everyday life. . . ."✍

Student Model

Writer Tim Capewell based his sketch on someone he had heard about from a friend. The name of the character and the situation are totally fictional. Throughout this sketch, you will note one basic personality trait clearly developed.

The opening lines present images of a man "bigger (and clumsier) than life."

The sketch focuses on Broderick's manner of driving.

Note that the narrator provides many actions, details, and explanations.

Broderick Monroe

Broderick Monroe was a huge man, and wherever he happened to be, became his own private china closet. It was as though Monroe had been designed for a world of different boundaries. His collar always appeared too tight. He was forever stuffing his shirttail back inside his pants, a few minutes later only to have it once more dangling visible below his suit jacket. The laces on his shoes were always untied. He always seemed to cause a scene without knowing that he was doing anything wrong.

A sweep of an arm would send a lamp crashing to the floor; a friendly slap on the back would nearly drive a person to his knees. His employees lived in fear of Monroe's friendly invitation to, "C'mon and take a ride with me." A drive across town with Monroe behind the wheel was a one-of-a-kind experience. Veterans at the office made up excuses for not accepting a ride from their boss. New employees didn't know any better.

Monroe drove with perfect faith that other drivers somehow could read every twist of his wild mind, and luckily they usually did. He'd carry on conversations that frequently required him to take both hands off the steering wheel to make a point. Monroe set a course of his own making unaware of any impact he was having on the cursing, scrambling drivers trying to get out of his way. Monroe's passengers generally emerged from a trip with him shaken and determined never to get into a car with Monroe again under any circumstance.

Monroe was indeed one of the chosen few. His baby face never showed any signs of confusion or doubt. His sleep was never disturbed by nightmares. Like a hurricane or a tornado or some other force of nature, Monroe simply was. You could love him or hate him, but you could not change him anymore than you could change the tides.

Professional Model

Character sketches are often part of a longer piece of writing. This model, for example, comes from the novel *Where the Red Fern Grows*. Note how the main character in this sketch thinks and acts completely for himself. There is no commentary or explanation from a narrator or someone else in the story. (From *Where the Red Fern Grows* by Wilson Rawls, copyright © 1961 by Woodrow Wilson Rawls. Copyright © 1961 Curtis Publishing Co. Used by permission of Bantam Books, a division of Bantam Doubleday Dell Publishing Group, Inc.)

Where the Red Fern Grows

Note that this sketch starts right in the middle of the action.

After making a few faces at myself, I put my thumbs in my ears and was making mule ears when two old women came by. They stopped and stared at me. I stared back. As they turned to go on their way, I heard one of them say something to the other. The words were hard to catch, but I did hear one word: "Wild." As I said before, they couldn't help it, they were womenfolks.

As I turned to leave, my eyes again fell on the overalls and the bolts of cloth. I thought of my mother, father, and sisters. Here was an opportunity to make amends for leaving home without telling anyone.

I entered the store. I bought a pair of overalls for Papa. After telling the storekeeper how big my mother and sisters were, I bought several yards of cloth. I also bought a large sack of candy.

Glancing down at my bare feet, the storekeeper said, "I have some good shoes."

I told him I didn't need any shoes.

The brief conversation between the boy and the shopkeeper reveals something about the boy's character.

He asked if that would be all.

I nodded.

He added up the bill. I handed him my ten dollars. He gave me my change.

After wrapping up the bundles, he helped me put them in my sack. Lifting it to my shoulder, I turned and left the store.

Out on the street, I picked out a friendly looking old man and asked him where the depot was. He told me to go down to the last street and turn right, go as far as I could, and I couldn't miss it. I thanked him and started on my way.

Leaving the main part of town, I started up a long street through the residential section. I had never seen so many beautiful houses, and they were all different colors. The lawns were neat and clean and looked like green carpets. I saw a man pushing some kind of mowing machine. I stopped to watch the whirling blades. He gawked at me. I hurried on.

Decide what dominant feeling or quality about the character is established in this sketch.

I heard a lot of shouting and laughing ahead of me. Not wanting to miss anything, I walked a little faster. I saw what was making the noise. More kids than I had ever seen were playing around a big red brick building. I thought some rich man lived there and was giving a party for his children. Walking up to the edge of the playground, I stopped to watch. . . .

One boy, spying me standing on the corner, came over. Looking me up and down, he asked, "Do you go to school here?"

I said, "School?"

He said, "Sure. School. What did you think it was?"

"We are leaving the old house on the corner
And the yard on which it stands and extends
From the next-door neighbor's driveway
To the tall pine trees . . . "   —Lisa Larson

Memory Poem

A memory poem shares a dominant feeling about a
certain time or place from the writer's past. The
writer listens with his or her heart as the poem
develops, selecting just the right words and images
to capture this feeling.

"What dreams are these . . ."

Discussion: Share a vivid personal memory in the form of a poem, focusing your attention on the emotional heart or core of the experience. Remember that in poetry special attention is generally given to specific words and phrases (rather than sentences and paragraphs) to convey a message or feeling. Provided below are basic guidelines to help you develop your poem. Also note the model poems following these guidelines. Additional information about writing poems can be found in the handbook. (Refer to "Poem" in the index.)

Searching and Selecting

1. **Selecting** • Think of a living memory as the starting point for your poem. This could be a memory of an event, a person, a place, an object, a dream, etc.

2. **Reviewing** • If you have trouble coming up with a subject, review your journal entries for ideas. Or write freely about a certain time in your life.

Generating the Text

3. **Noting** • Once you have a subject in mind, think of an interesting way to write about it. You might want to focus on a specific image (mental picture), feeling, or important idea related to the memory. Or, you might want to do all of these things. The choice is yours.

4. **Collecting** • Write freely and rapidly about the memory if you feel a need to collect your thoughts about it. Doing this may also help you think of interesting ways to shape your poem.

Writing and Revising

5. **Writing** • The way your poem develops is really up to you. It may, for example, turn out to be a list of words and phrases as they freely come to mind one after another. Then again, you may express your thoughts and feelings in complete ideas. Or, if you have a general plan in mind, you may develop your poem more carefully and selectively in another way— perhaps according to the guidelines of a traditional form of poetry like the ballad.

6. **Revising** • Review the first draft of your poem, noting words and ideas that you like and those you will change. Revise and refine your poem accordingly.

Evaluating

Does the poem form a meaningful whole, moving smoothly from the opening words and phrases to the final idea or image?

Has proper attention been given to specific word choice, details, figures of speech . . . ?

Will readers appreciate the treatment of the memory in this poem?

Does the poem leave readers with a lasting impression or feeling?

Help File: Try reworking a recent journal entry, story, or essay into a poem.

Student Model

Student writer Ingrid Clemen shares a personal moment in her free-verse poem "Breaking the Calm." She captures a simple but satisfying summer experience through the effective use of sensory details.

In the opening section, sensory details establish a peaceful, calm tone.

A sense of concern changes the tone of the poem.

Breaking the Calm

it was almost dark
light was just beginning to reflect off the water
the planks of the pier shook as I ran over them
I stared out at the calm water and waited for my dad
the air was hot and muggy
and gnats were starting to fly around my ears
I could hear the waves peacefully lap onto shore
the boat rocked gently in the water
my grandpa named the boat *Clementine*
but I could hardly see the lettering

it was a warm night so we had decided to swim
        to our boat
instead of taking the old beat-up rowboat
but I was deathly afraid of seaweed
            maybe it would strangle me
            maybe there were bugs and worms in it
splash!
I was pushed in by my dad
after swallowing some water I caught my breath
and raced him to the small deck at the back of our boat
forgetting all about the seaweed

Student Model

In the following poem, writer Jessica Feeney presents a dreamlike picture of her mother, the gardener. In offering the reader this small slice of life, the author shares much more. That's the nature of poetry.

The writer effectively captures her mother at work in her own special world.

A sense of calm is created through a series of descriptive images (pictures).

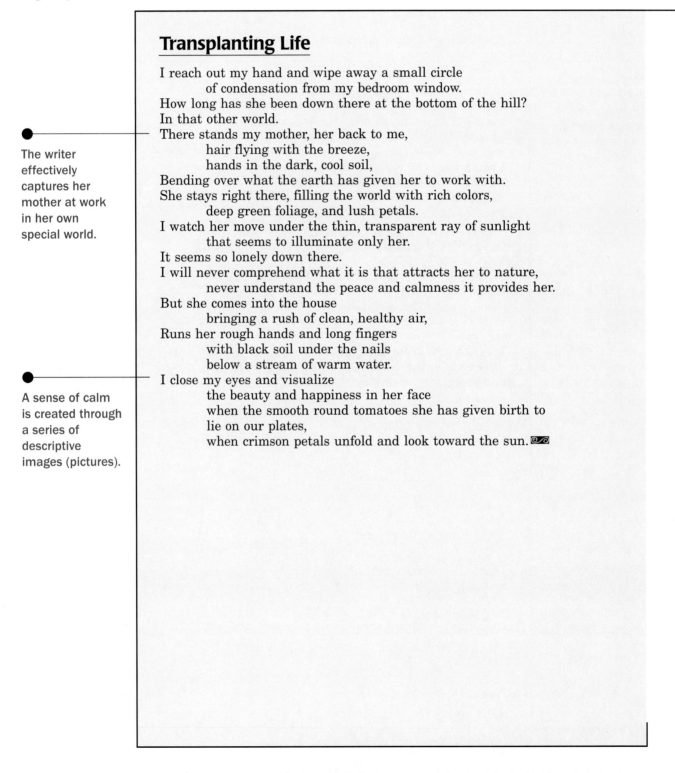

Transplanting Life

I reach out my hand and wipe away a small circle
     of condensation from my bedroom window.
How long has she been down there at the bottom of the hill?
In that other world.
There stands my mother, her back to me,
     hair flying with the breeze,
     hands in the dark, cool soil,
Bending over what the earth has given her to work with.
She stays right there, filling the world with rich colors,
     deep green foliage, and lush petals.
I watch her move under the thin, transparent ray of sunlight
     that seems to illuminate only her.
It seems so lonely down there.
I will never comprehend what it is that attracts her to nature,
     never understand the peace and calmness it provides her.
But she comes into the house
     bringing a rush of clean, healthy air,
Runs her rough hands and long fingers
     with black soil under the nails
     below a stream of warm water.
I close my eyes and visualize
     the beauty and happiness in her face
     when the smooth round tomatoes she has given birth to
     lie on our plates,
     when crimson petals unfold and look toward the sun.

Student Model

In this poem, writer Lisa Prusinski investigates her own feeling toward a childhood friend. The poem is deceivingly simple and effective. Note how the writer pulls you along from spring to fall, from trying to make a friend, to trying to get rid of an enemy, to finally realizing how that person was really a friend after all. (This poem originally appeared in the December/January 1992 issue of *Merlyn's Pen: The National Magazine of Student Writing*. It is reprinted by permission of *Merlyn's Pen*.)

The poem has a very personal tone, as if written directly to Steven.

The writer includes a number of visual details, making it easy to *see* Steven.

Using a detail from the poem's beginning, the writer comes full circle for a strong ending.

To Steven, My Childhood Friend

In June we went crayfishing;
You broke my pail.
You made me red-faced and angry
Cheating in Monopoly,
Scribbling in my coloring book.
I tried hard to be your friend,
But you wrecked my Lego house in one blow.

For your birthday, a mud puddle day in July,
We gave you a T-shirt that read
"Joe Cool"
Next to a picture of Snoopy;
You lived up to it well
Standing on a swing like a mighty warrior.
Never were you content with peace—
Blocking the sidewalk with your Bigwheel
Creating havoc.
I wished and wished that you would go away,
And late one afternoon
I heard the rumor goin' round the block
That your dad was transferred
To Indiana
I rejoiced:
No more broken Barbie Dolls or fixed games of tag.

For the remaining part of that dusty August
The neighborhood was quiet and still;
We were restless and antsy,
Only hushed Monopoly games
And calm-weathered days in Lego-land.
No more art contests or anticipated Bigwheel warfare.
No one knocking on our doors
With invitations
To crayfish anymore.

Student Model

In this poem, student writer Lisa Larson uses the house in which she grew up as a focal point. We learn of her mixed feelings about moving away, how sad and unnerving it is for her. But we also learn of her parents' struggle to find better employment and arrange for the family to be together every day, not just on the weekends. (This poem originally appeared in the April/May 1991 issue of *Merlyn's Pen: The National Magazine of Student Writing*. It is reprinted by permission of *Merlyn's Pen*.)

The writer describes her childhood home and neighborhood and the experiences she had growing up there.

This poem is written in the present tense, but it also looks back into the past and ahead to the future.

Announcement

We are leaving the old house on the corner
And the yard on which it stands and extends
From the next-door neighbor's driveway
To the tall pine trees,
Which we would play house under
And climb,
Only to get our hands full of sap,
Which Mother would clean off with special soap
That made our hands smell.

We are leaving this tall green house
With steep stairs up to the bedrooms
And on whose porch we had thrift sales,
So we could earn enough money
To go down to the
Hardware store
And buy a toy
Or go to the corner store
To buy candy, Popsicles or drumsticks,
Which we'd eat on the way home
As we walked down the road by the feedmill
Which was freshly paved—
Where we'd ride our bikes in good weather
And have races
With the wind whipping on our faces
As we gasped for breath.

We are leaving our house in Fall Creek
And bidding farewell
To the houses across the street
And to the bar down by the creek
Where drunks would stagger onto the street
Which led to the train tracks by our house—
Where rumbling trains would sound their whistle
And shake the house as they passed
Making the pictures on the wall shake
And our beds vibrate
Causing Mother to be afraid
The house would cave in.

Pay attention to the way the writer tells little stories within the poem. The whole poem is built upon these striking, individual recollections.

We are loading the truck with furniture
And clearing out our rooms
Where we used to stare out the window
Pretending to be detectives
Saying "Hi!" to passersby
And writing down information
In our little notebooks
Enjoying the thrill of jumping away
Before they could see us
But scared stiff when a man with a paper bag,
That looked like a gun was inside,
Walked across the street
And stared right up at us
But was gone by the time we sent Father out.

We will no more hear the siren scream
From the fire station down the street
And run outside
In the heat of a summer day
To watch
And see which way the fire engines would go
Counting the number of whistles in a row
Indicating the size of the fire.
We will never again attend
The fishing contest
At the pond by the park
And have the chance of winning a prize
For the second-place fish
Which was one-half inch shorter than the first—
As I once did.

The writer repeats "We are leaving . . ." to add rhythm and deep feeling to the poem.

We are leaving our house
Because Father has finished school
And has gotten a job in Minneapolis
Where he will be a computer operator
for Abbot Northwestern,
And because Father is lonely and needs us
For he has been living alone
In a one-room apartment
And walking too many blocks to work
Through the slush and cold,
Visiting us by bus on weekends
For we have only one car.

I will miss this old house
And my purple room
Which my family painted
One summer as a surprise
While I was off at camp.

Professional Model

In this model, Naomi Long Madgett assumes the role of her aunt, Octavia Long, in a memory poem about going to school. Perhaps you know of someone from your past that you would like to honor (or assume) in a poem. ("Teacher" is reprinted from *Octavia and Other Poems* © 1988 [Third World Press] by Naomi Long Madgett. It is used by permission of Naomi Long Madgett.)

Notice how the warm interaction between the subject of the poem and the "sweet, high voices of children" contrasts with the dismal images early in the poem.

Teacher

Hatless, you trudge through alabaster days
       over the railroad tracks
       raised above the level
       of all but the severest floods
to your fifth grade class at Lincoln School
       raw winds biting your naked fingers
       dust searing your eyes.

The furnace is slow to heat
and the only light available
comes through the windows.

       Mama's first grade classroom
       on the floor below
       is even colder, but by ten o'clock
       both will be quite comfortable.

The sweet, high voices of children
       cheer you.
The adoration in their eyes
       warms the dismal atmosphere.
You touch your light to their dark lamps.

Winter, 1909-1910
Guthrie, Oklahoma

"Meredith, Sarah, and I are sitting in the cafeteria. Meredith's chowing down, I'm stirring ice around in a bowl, and Sarah's watching us.
*'So what **are** bacon bits made of?' Sarah asks.*
'We have this conversation every day. . . .' "
—Denise Langevine

Dialogue Writing

In a dialogue, a writer creates a conversation that sounds like it could have actually taken place. An effective dialogue reveals something significant about the speakers' personalities.

Say something!

Discussion: Create a dialogue (conversation) between two individuals discussing a topic of your own choosing. Base your dialogue on real conversations you have had or heard (changing names and/or altering the situation to protect the innocent), or start from scratch and create something totally new and unexpected. What the individuals say should give some insight into their personalities and makeup. Make sure that your dialogue forms a complete whole with a beginning, a middle, and an end. Provided below are basic guidelines to help you develop your writing. Also note the model dialogues following these guidelines.

Searching and Selecting

1. **Reviewing** • Think of actual conversations you have had or overheard that could serve as potential starting points for your dialogue. (Suppose you and your brother or sister had a heated discussion about each other's friends the other night. There is the starting point for a dialogue. Simply change the characters in some way, alter the nature of the discussion a bit, and see what develops.)

2. **Listing** • Or think in terms of situations that might generate interesting conversations: a new student in a school and his or her locker mate; two seasoned employees at a local fast-food restaurant. With the help of a classmate or writing group, create a list of these situations. (With a good idea for your dialogue in mind, go right to your first draft if you wish. Otherwise, refer to "Generating the Text.")

Generating the Text

3. **Noting** • Think about the speakers in your dialogue. Who are they? What will they be like and how will they talk? What is the subject of their conversation?

4. **Focusing** • You might also think about the way you will present the dialogue. How is it going to start? Where is it going to take place (if that is important)? Will you need to provide background information? (See the models for ideas.)

Writing and Revising

5. **Writing** • Write the first draft of the dialogue freely as the characters' words naturally come to mind—or follow any planning and organizing you may have done. (Don't be surprised if your dialogue takes on a life of its own and takes you in a new direction.)

6. **Revising** • Read your first draft aloud to get a general sense of the sound and flow of the words and ideas. Have someone else read your draft as well. Revise and refine accordingly.

Evaluating

Does each speaker have a distinctive voice?

Do the speakers' remarks seem believable within the context of the dialogue?

Is the dialogue related to a specific idea or topic?

Help File: Write a brief character sketch (paragraph) for each speaker to establish some background information about his or her personality.

Student Model

Sometimes what we say is not as important as what we don't say. In this model dialogue written by Denise Langevine, see if you can detect any hidden meanings lying somewhere behind the actual conversation that takes place. ("Cafeteria" first appeared in *Scroll '91*, a literary publication of the Holton-Arms School in Bethesda, Maryland. It is reprinted with permission.)

Cafeteria

Meredith, Sarah, and I are sitting in the cafeteria. Meredith's chowing down, I'm stirring ice around in a bowl, and Sarah's watching us.

"So what *are* bacon bits made of?" Sarah asks.

"We have this conversation every day. It's soy, they're made of soy, *not* kidney beans! Now my ice tastes like salt. I want some more."

"Chewing ice is a sign of sexual frustration," Meredith says.

"I heard that before, but I don't believe it," I say, craving ice.

"Pooja told me that in eighth grade," Meredith says.

"Yeah, I remember, at her slumber party," Sarah says, reaching over to pick up Meredith's glazed cinnamon apple tart dessert thing.

"I HATE when you do that. *Why* do you do that?" I scream.

"What?" Sarah and Meredith ask.

"You just picked up her apple thing and just licked it like some kind of barbarian! It'd be different if you were gonna eat it, but you don't even like them!"

"There are a hundred more over there. It would take two seconds to get another one," Sarah screams.

"So?"

"So."

"How do you know that Meredith wasn't just about to stop eating her stupid salad and decide to eat that apple thing? Maybe she *really* wants it right now! You don't know!"

"So . . . I can just get her another one. What's the big deal? Why do you always think you have to defend other people? If Meredith doesn't care, what's the big deal?"

Meredith looks up from her salad. She smiles.

"So if someone was being murdered in the street, you wouldn't do anything because you don't want to defend other people, and . . ."

"Taking an apple pie is not the same as killing someone."

"Well . . . that's only your opinion. Maybe it's the same to me. What? So I'm wrong because I don't think the same as you? Maybe I'm right and you're wrong!"

"Shut up!"

Meredith's laughing hysterically, and some Lower Schoolers come over and sit down.

"The thing is, you just can't do that your whole life. You can't just take stuff and *assume* it's okay."

"You sound like my mom. Meredith doesn't even want it," Sarah says.

"Not really," Meredith says.

"Seeeeeeee?" Sarah gloats. ✍

Note how the speakers' personalities take shape during the dialogue.

Ask yourself if the writer has effectively captured the way high-school girls might argue a point.

If it's clear who is talking, it's not necessary to always include an "I said" or "she asked."

Student Model

In this model, a dialogue develops between a younger brother, who is in the midst of an "educational crisis," and his older sister. The interchanges between the brother and sister provide insights into their personalities. (Note that this dialogue is written in script form.)

The opening lines establish a semihumorous tone for the dialogue.

Note how Liz's comments reflect her amazement at her brother's situation.

As the dialogue continues, the brother's "story" becomes more unbelievable.

What Can I Say?

Liz: You are in deep trouble, Little Bro. So what are you going to tell Mom?

Billy: Mom? What about Dad?

Liz: Dad? He's easy. But, you know Mom.

Billy: Yeah, she'll make me feel awful. And . . .

Liz: But, how could you fail? I don't think Blodgett's failed two people in the last twenty years.

Billy: You sure are a big help.

Liz: Why don't you try to see if Blodgett will let you make up the work?

Billy: I already asked. He said "no."

Liz: How much work do you owe?

Billy: Kind of all of it.

Liz: All of it! You didn't hand in anything the whole marking period?

Billy: Yeah, pretty much.

Liz: What do you mean, "pretty much"? You either did or you didn't.

Billy: I did all of the in-class work, but no important assignments.

Liz: You went the entire marking period and never handed in a single assignment. How could you do that?

Billy: I just sort of got behind, and thought I could catch up, and you know Blodgett never says anything.

Liz: What did you tell him when you went to see him?

Billy: I said that I owed some assignments and I wondered if he'd let me do some extra work to make them up. And he said, how did I think I could make up so much work right before grades were to come out.

Liz: And what did you say?

Billy: I said well maybe I could write a book report or something.

Liz: Oh, real good!

Billy: And he got a little upset. And then, uh, he sort of asked me why I hadn't done the work, and, well, I said I'd been really upset this term.

Liz: You'd been upset? About what, pray tell?

Billy: I said, you know, that I, that I'd been having some real tough personal problems, a death in the family.

Liz: What? Who died?

Billy: Uh, grandma.

Liz: Come on! And what did he say?

Billy: Well, he, you know, I mean, he said he wondered why he hadn't heard about this before . . .

Liz: And?

Billy: I don't think he bought it at all . . . and, what can I say?

Liz: Obviously not a whole lot. I don't believe you!

Billy: So, uh, I don't really think he's gonna let me make up the work.

Liz: You are incredible, just downright incredible.

Billy: So, what am I going to tell Mom and Dad?

Liz: That, Little Bro, is one very interesting question. ✍

Professional Model

The following dialogue presents a mini-story of sorts about two youngsters meeting a newcomer in the neighborhood. Note how smoothly the conversation moves from one speaker to the next. This model is an excerpt from *To Kill a Mockingbird* by Harper Lee. (Copyright © 1960 by Harper Lee. Reprinted by permission of HarperCollins Publishers.)

The opening paragraph sets the scene for the dialogue.

Note that the dialogue helps us learn something about the characters.

The characters are all children, and they *sound* like children when they speak.

"I'm Charles Baker Harris"

Early one morning as we were beginning our day's play in the back yard, Jem and I heard something next door in Miss Rachel Haverford's collard patch. We went to the wire fence to see if there was a puppy—Miss Rachel's rat terrier was expecting—instead we found someone sitting looking at us. Sitting down, he wasn't much higher than the collards. We stared at him until he spoke:

"Hey."

"Hey yourself," said Jem pleasantly.

"I'm Charles Baker Harris," he said. "I can read."

"So what?" I said.

"I just thought you'd like to know I can read. You got anything needs readin' I can do it. . . ."

"How old are you," asked Jem, "four-and-a-half?"

"Goin' on seven."

"Shoot no wonder, then," said Jem, jerking his thumb at me. "Scout yonder's been readin' ever since she was born, and she ain't even started to school yet. You look right puny for goin' on seven."

"I'm little but I'm old," he said.

Jem brushed his hair back to get a better look. "Why don't you come over, Charles Baker Harris?" he said. "Lord, what a name."

" 's not any funnier'n yours. Aunt Rachel says your name's Jeremy Atticus Finch."

Jem scowled. "I'm big enough to fit mine," he said. "Your name's longer'n you are. Bet it's a foot longer."

"Folks call me Dill," said Dill, struggling under the fence.

"Do better if you go over it instead of under it," I said. "Where'd you come from?"

Dill was from Meridian, Mississippi, was spending the summer with his aunt, Miss Rachel, and would be spending every summer in Maycomb from now on. His family was from Maycomb County originally. His mother worked for a photographer in Meridian, had entered his picture in a Beautiful Child contest and won five dollars. She gave the money to Dill, who went to the picture show twenty times on it.

"Don't have any picture shows here, except Jesus ones in the courthouse sometimes," said Jem. "Ever see anything good?"

Dill had seen *Dracula*, a revelation that moved Jem to eye him with the beginning of respect. "Tell it to us," he said. . . . ✒

Reflective Writing

"As the bus filled with passengers, the driver turned and told her to give up her seat and move on back in the bus. She sat still. The driver got up and shouted, 'MOVE IT!' She sat still." —Robert Fulghum

Essay of Illustration

In an essay of illustration, a writer uses a personal experience to prove a point or make a statement. This type of writing usually reveals something important about the writer's view of life.

Writing in Search of Meaning

Discussion: Write an essay in which you use an experience in your life (or in the life of a friend or an acquaintance) to illustrate an idea or to make a statement. Be sure you know enough details about the incident (or have access to information about it) to present a "telling" story. Read the models and then follow the guidelines below to help you develop your writing.

Searching and Selecting

1. **Searching** • To start thinking about possible stories, list five emotions you have felt (fear, jealousy, joy, and so on). List five principles you think are important (loyalty, justice, truth, and so on). List five personal characteristics (courage, prejudice, honesty, and so on).

2. **Selecting** • From your lists, select three items that you've seen illustrated in your own or someone else's experiences. Free-write a few minutes on each experience, focusing on telling each story. Then choose the most interesting and meaningful story.

   Special Note: Use good judgment when selecting a subject. Avoid hurting anyone's feelings or embarrassing someone in your writing.

Generating the Text

3. **Recording** • Continue writing freely about your subject, recording all of your thoughts and feelings as they come to mind.

4. **Collecting** • If necessary, collect additional details to make the story vivid. (Refer to "Writing, About an event" in your handbook index.)

5. **Focusing** • Review your recording and collecting to make sure you have enough facts and details to tell your story. Also ask yourself what point the story illustrates. (See "Help File.")

Writing and Revising

6. **Writing** • As you write, focus on telling the story so that it will clearly communicate the main idea or concept you are attempting to illustrate.

7. **Refining** • Revise your writing so it's clear, interesting, and accurate. Ask two classmates to read your essay and tell you why they think the story is important. Revise as needed.

Evaluating

?······?

Does the story effectively illustrate an idea or a point?

Did any new meanings surface during the writing?

Will readers identify with the story?

Help File: If you get stuck finding the true focus of a story—figuring out what it illustrates—ask why the story is important to you. Why do you remember it? What details are most vivid? What do you feel when you think about it? Then shape your writing accordingly.

Student Model

Tiffanie Wiese's story illustrates the power of love in the midst of poverty. (The following essay originally appeared in the April 1992 issue of *High School Writer*. It is reprinted by permission.)

Can't Buy Love

Money can't buy you everything. Not only that, but money can't buy you important things such as love. When I was a small child, no matter how poor we were, I never realized it because there was so much love in our house.

When we didn't have enough to eat, my brother would go and steal food just so we could eat. He would risk arrest rather than see us go hungry. If my brother had had the money to buy us food, we probably wouldn't have realized how much he loved us. He risked himself time and again because he loved us so much.

When I was in elementary school, the kids would tease me because of the clothes that I wore. The clothes were my brother's hand-me-downs. My brother was in the sixth grade then. I never told him because I didn't want him to worry any more than he already worried about us.

One day, as soon as we got off the bus, my brother grabbed me by the arm and started yelling at me for not telling him about it. Apparently, he'd seen me getting teased at school. I thought he was so mad that he was going to hit me. Instead, he started crying and he gave me a hug. That same night, he went out and got a paper route so that I wouldn't have to wear hand-me-downs ever again.

Even now, we don't have a lot of money. We still have to buy Kingston and other store-brand products. We hardly ever have extra money, but we still have a lot of love. ✑

The writer's manner of speaking throughout the essay is simple, direct, and powerful.

Student Model

In the following essay, student writer Mike Varveris shares a story about a classmate to illustrate the word "alienation." Notice that this disturbing story is developed in great detail from start to finish.

Alienation

The opening paragraph introduces the writer's subject.

Alienation can occur in many different situations, and I personally know that it happens every day in high school. I know a boy named George who was teased by a group of jerks in my sophomore gym class because of his strange appearance and timidity. I know of one experience that illustrates alienation in that gym class better than any other.

Once, before gym class, George walked into the locker room almost inaudibly; the only noise he made was the methodical dragging of his feet. He looked as if he had slept in his wrinkled clothes. His hair was an uncombed mess, his shirt wasn't tucked in his pants in back, and both of his shoes were untied. He mumbled something—I think maybe "Hi"—as he passed me, and then went over to open his locker. While he was fingering the combination lock, the jerks of the class came in. George gave them a nervous look over his shoulder, and then threw open his locker. He ran his hands over the mound of gym clothes inside and quickly, almost viciously, pulled them out, seemingly not caring that half of the clothes collapsed onto the floor. As he bent over to pick them up, the jerks surrounded him, hurling taunts such as, "Hey, Georgie, Momma really dressed you up pretty today," and "Hey, George, you still blowin' that trumpet on Friday nights?" George didn't look up at them, but waited until the jerks stopped crowding him before he picked up the remainder of his gym clothes and scuttled silently away. He hid behind the lockers and didn't begin putting his soiled gym clothes on until all of the jerks had finished dressing and had gone into the gym.

The writer describes George and relates his gym-class experiences.

When he finally entered the gym and sat down, waiting for attendance to be taken, I heard a few whistles coming from the jerks behind me. George acted as if he hadn't heard them, but in the way he sighed deeply and then balanced his head on his knees, I could tell that he was only pretending. After roll call, captains for basketball teams were picked. George volunteered by halfway raising his hand, but the teacher overlooked him. Each captain then picked teams, and George ended up being the last kid picked. It turned out that George was on my team, and he acted very enthused about it all. Throughout the beginning of the first game, George played his best, and once even managed to steal the basketball. A few minutes later, George eagerly motioned with both arms for me to pass the ball to him. I did, and, as soon as he got hold of the ball, he shot. However, he missed, and within seconds, the jerks surrounded him again and almost crucified him with their verbal abuse, telling him to keep his hands to himself. For the rest of the period, George stayed away from the basketball and kept out of everyone's way. I was about to pass the ball to him again later, but he peered at me with fearful eyes and quickly turned around on his heels.

The final paragraph illustrates alienation so dramatically, the writer does not even need to repeat the word.

George lagged behind as everyone filed into the locker room after the class was dismissed. There, he waited for the crowd of jerks around his locker to disperse. When an opening appeared, George squeezed through it and began undressing. The jerks started jeering at him and shouted, "Muscles, muscles," when George pulled off his T-shirt, revealing his pale, rib-lined chest which looked like that of an old man. He continued taking off his gym clothes and was putting on his wrinkled outfit, when one of the jerks threw a pair of ragged underwear at him. It landed on his waist, and George didn't even throw it off. After quietly staring at it for a few seconds, George slid along the bench underneath the underwear and let it slowly drop to rest on the bench. George tried his best to hold in the pain, but he breathed irregularly, as if between sobs. He finished dressing and walked to the hallway leading out of the locker room. As the bell rang, the kid who threw the underwear at him yelled, "See ya' tomorrow, George," and shoved him in the back, right between the shoulder blades. George passed me, and, as he did, I saw the wet mark of a tear meandering down his cheek toward his trembling, chapped lips. ✍

Professional Model

In this model, Robert Fulghum first reflects upon being told as a child to sit still, and then follows with a story about a woman named Rosa Parks who did just that, and made a powerful point. (From *It Was On Fire When I Lay Down On It* by Robert Fulghum. Copyright © 1988, 1989 by Robert Fulghum. Reprinted by permission of Villard Books, a division of Random House, Inc.)

"SIT STILL—"

Note that the author addresses sitting still in a somewhat playful manner in the first paragraph.

"SIT STILL—JUST SIT STILL!" My mother's voice. Again and again. Teachers in school said it, too. And I, in my turn, have said it to my children and my students. Why do adults say this? Can't recall any child ever really sitting still just because some adults said to. That explains why several "sit stills" are often followed by "SIT DOWN AND SHUT UP!" or "SHUT UP AND SIT DOWN!" My mother once used both versions back to back, and I, smart-mouth that I was, asked her just which she wanted me to do first—shut up or sit down? My mother gave me that look. The one that meant she knew she would go to jail if she killed me, but it just might be worth it. At such a moment an adult will say very softly, one syllable at a time: "Get—out—of—my—sight." Any kid with half a brain will get up and go. Then the parent will sit very still.

Paragraph two suggests that sitting can be action oriented.

Sitting still can be powerful stuff, though. It is on my mind as I write this on the first day of December in 1988, the anniversary of a moment when someone sat still and lit the fuse to social dynamite. On this day in 1955, a forty-two-year-old woman was on her way home from work. Getting on a public bus, she paid her fare and sat down on the first vacant seat. It was good to sit down—her feet were tired. As the bus filled with passengers, the driver turned and told her to give up her seat and move on back in the bus. She sat still. The driver got up and shouted, "MOVE IT!" She sat still. Passengers grumbled, cursed her, pushed at her. Still she sat. So the driver got off the bus, called the police, and they came to haul her off to jail and into history.

By sitting still, Ms. Parks helped desegregate the bus system in Montgomery, Alabama.

Rosa Parks. Not an activist or a radical. Just a quiet, conservative, churchgoing woman with a nice family and a decent job as a seamstress. For all the eloquent phrases that have been turned about her place in the flow of history, she did not get on that bus looking for trouble or trying to make a statement. Going home was all she had in mind, like everybody else. She was anchored to her seat by her own dignity. . . . And all she knew to do was to sit still. ✎

"There's a saying in my language: 'The old way is the best way.' " —Fariba Nawa

Dialogue of Ideas

In a dialogue of ideas, two real or imagined characters discuss an important, timely subject. The writer can discuss a subject from many different points of view during the dialogue.

Can we talk...?

Discussion: Create a dialogue between two people in which you discuss an important issue or argue for or against a particular point of view. This dialogue may be between yourself and someone you are familiar with (a parent), between yourself and someone you are not so familiar with (the president), or between two completely different people. Think of this dialogue as a give-and-take of ideas in which each person makes clear his or her own position and responds to the other person's ideas. Provided below are basic guidelines to help you develop your writing. Also note the model dialogues following these guidelines.

Searching and Selecting

1. **Reviewing** • Think about actual discussions or disagreements you have had with a parent, friend, or someone else.

2. **Searching** • Consider issues, events, and requirements related to school life as well as life on the outside. If you have trouble thinking of potential subjects, brainstorm for ideas.

Generating the Text

3. **Identifying** • In a sentence or two, state the issue or topic of your work so it is clear in your mind before you start writing your dialogue.

4. **Gathering** • You will want to collect plenty of facts and details related to the subject before you start your dialogue. This will be especially important if you are discussing a topic for the first time.

Writing and Revising

5. **Writing** • Write your dialogue freely, letting the discussion develop naturally. Keep your writing going as long as possible until the discussion comes to a natural stopping point. (This does not mean that everything has to be resolved by the end of the dialogue.)

6. **Refining** • Review, revise, and refine your writing before sharing it with your readers. (Refer to the Proofreader's Guide in the handbook when you are ready to proofread your work.)

Evaluating

?••••**?**   Has the subject been explored in a thorough fashion?

Have the speakers addressed (rather than ignored) specific points of disagreement?

Does the dialogue form a meaningful whole, moving forward from one point to the next?

Help File: If you have trouble finding a topic, review your school paper, local newspaper, or a national news magazine.

Student Model

What kinds of intimate conversations do teenagers have? Here, two friends from different ethnic backgrounds discuss the role of women in their families, communities, and high school. Fariba Nawa is an Afghan-born Muslim and Nicci Jones is an African-American; both are 17 years old. (Reprinted from *YO! (Youth Outlook)*, the Journal of [San Francisco] Bay Area Teen Life [September 1991], published by the Center for Integration and Improvement of Journalism at San Francisco State University and Pacific News Service.)

The speakers present their positions and reveal the issue under discussion.

Sexism—Two young women discuss cultural differences

Fariba: My Afghan culture is extremely sexist from a Western point of view. But in my community, there's no such thing as sexism. Afghan women are mainly Muslims. They accept their roles as housewives and let their husbands be the heads of the house. Islam doesn't say men are superior to women, but it does give each a role.

Most Muslim women who live in the Muslim countries see no need for change. It's when they come to this part of the world that they feel trapped. I feel like a prime example. I live two lives: one at home within my community and one outside in this society.

Nicci: As an African-American living in Union City, I feel like an outsider because of the way I think. It's strange, because in the black community women are so much in the forefront. But so many women get so desperate in the way they need men, that they're starting to cut back on their values and strengths and just become docile. I'm not like that. Black men feel put down and very oppressed as men in this society, and so a black man likes to come home to a woman who is always nice and gentle, so he can feel like a man in his house. I don't think I could do that. It's hard, because I plan to be successful, and so many black men are scared of successful black women.

Fariba: When I came here from Afghanistan, I realized I didn't have to live out the role I was given. At first I rebelled against the rules of my culture. I refused to do my girly chores, like bringing tea to the guests, and constantly talked about how Muslim women needed to change their submissiveness. My parents understood, but my small community didn't. They started to talk about me and how "Americanized" I'd become. I saw that all the gossip was hurting my family, so I stopped talking so "radical."

But there are certain things I will never accept in my culture. For example, I want to go away to college, and most Afghans think that I can't take care of myself. But I won't give in. On the other hand, Muslim men like to offer protection and that's something I can accept. I don't get defensive like an American woman might about how she can take care of herself. The men aren't just satisfying their egos by protecting a woman; they're also doing their job as men.

The writers use questions and answers to make their positions clear.

Nicci: Do you see your situation as a curse or a blessing?

Fariba: I see it as a blessing. I'd rather be desperate and miserable knowing too much than content not knowing what's going on.

Nicci: Why is change so impossible?

Fariba: There's a saying in my language: "The old way is the best way." Authority of any kind isn't challenged. Whatever authorities (usually elders) say is considered to be right and is respected. As a result, almost everyone's a follower. If you're a leader who goes against authority, you're ostracized.

Nicci: I'm conflicted because I really love men and want to get married and have children, but I also love my beliefs. I think it would be a hard struggle to find someone who could really deal with me.

Fariba: And yet you might not want to marry outside of your race, because you want that cultural tie.

Nicci: Right. I really want to become a strong part of the black community, and I would like to find a partner who feels the same. I think to find everything that I need could be really hard. People settle, but I can't settle.

Fariba: That's a problem for me also. Most Islamic men want someone who'll literally obey them. Most Muslim women who come here change like me and become more liberated. So most of the men here look for wives back in the Muslim countries. Although I would let a man play out his role to protect me, I refuse to obey anyone. I call that oppression. But I don't exactly feel like a free woman in this society either. I find men's view of women as objects sickening, and I blame the media for degrading women. In almost every music video I see, there's a half-nude woman parading up and down.

Nicci: A lot of women think that's admiration. It's like the only way a lot of men can admire women is by degrading them, giving them wolf calls on the streets. I'd rather have a "Good morning, how are you?" or a nice look, not "Ooh, baby, shake that, bring that over here." That's sick.

Fariba: It is sick. It's nice to get attention, but for me to have to wear sleazy clothes just to get attention is cheap. I think one of the biggest reasons women haven't overcome sexism is that they need men's approval.

One way is to tell guys off when they make dirty jokes about women. Even if they don't take you seriously, it makes you feel better.

My family has pretty much accepted me by now. We had a lot of conflicts, but they see that I'm well accomplished. It's the people in our community that are the problem. I stay away from them, which is the saddest part. Most of my friends are not Afghans, are non-Muslims. But I do want to hang out with other Muslims, because they know how I live, they know my life. So it's a conflict.

Nicci: I feel the exact same way. That's one reason why I'm going back East to college. A lot of black girls here, their biggest interest is trying to get with some guy. They couldn't care less about education. To hang out with them would be a joke, because that's not who I am.

People want me to be a certain way, and I can't be that certain way. Like my old boyfriend. He wanted me to be less of an individual. He wanted me to do what he wanted me to do. He wanted someone to understand him. And I think I understand him just as much as I need to.

Fariba: Will anyone ever understand us?

Nicci: I don't know. I'm waiting for the day I don't have to go around explaining myself. ☙

The writers compare and contrast their ideas to clarify them for the reader.

Their conflicts remain unresolved, but the girls seem to find support in knowing that they understand each other.

Professional Model

Verne Meyer writes a dialogue of ideas between two high-school kids arguing about whether it's more honorable to get a part-time job or play sports. Meyer sets the scene in the dairy section of a grocery store where Sam is stacking gallon cartons of milk into a refrigerator, and Phil has stopped by on his way to basketball practice. Notice that this piece tells a little story and includes stage directions to help readers imagine the action.

Playin' by the Rules

(Sam stands between the refrigerator and a cart with three cases of milk. He has emptied the first case and is starting on the second. Phil sits on the edge of a refrigerated food bin, duffel bag at his feet.)

Phil: You're sick, man. Haulin' out grocery bags, sweepin' the floor, smilin' at fat ladies who don't know your name . . . and don't care. Sick.

Sam: *(setting carton in refrigerator)* Yeah, well who's gonna buy my clothes? Help my mom pay rent? Give me a couple bucks to spend some Saturday night? What Santa Claus is gonna swoop down the chimney once a week to put 50 bucks in my wallet? Who? You?

Phil: *(picks up a package of cheese)* What's wrong with me? I get by.

Sam: Yeah, you get by all right. All you do is get by. Fact is, you're a specialist at gettin' by.

Phil: Hey, I enjoy myself. You're only a kid once . . . except you. You were born old.

(Phil laughs as he tosses the package up and tries to catch it behind his back; but Sam reaches out, grabs the package, and slaps it back in the bin.)

Sam: I was born to a mother who taught me that nobody owes me nothin'. And if I get the wants for somethin' I need—or don't need—she made me two hands to earn it.

(Sam resumes stacking.)

Phil: Earn it? On what? How much does Mr. Clean Hands, White Shirt, Jewel Grocery Store Man pay you to do his dirty work? Minimum wage? You can't earn nothin' on minimum wage.

Sam: How much you earnin', runnin' around a gym every afternoon, dressed in short pants that taxes out of MY minimum wage pay for? Chasin' a bouncin' ball I pay for? Listenin' to a grown man with a kid's whistle tell you when to jump, pass, shoot, and sit on the bench to WATCH? Shoot, Phil, my taxes even pay for HIM!

(Sam sets two empty cases on the cart and begins work on the third.)

Phil: *(short pause, watching Sam work)* That's it, ain't it?

Sam: What's it?

Phil: You're still corked off at Coach Williams for starting Dweeb instead of you.

Sam: *(Surprised, he stops.)* Man . . . that was months ago!

Phil: So you tore off the uniform and walked out.

Sam: *(angry, slams door of refrigerator)* Walked in. Walked IN! I walked out of the "playpen" where a guy with a whistle orders school boys around to win games that make HIM the big man in HIS life, and I walked IN to my own life where nobody wears a whistle, and where I play the

---

The conflict is introduced early.

The boys then argue back and forth, trying to get the better of each other.

real game of workin' hard, earnin' my own keep, and . . . oh, yeah, and payin' the taxes so little boys like you can run around in short pants, chase a ball, jump up and down, and get by.

Phil: Get by, huh?

Sam: Get by.

Phil: Well, hey. I don't care what you say, Sammie OLD Man, some of us— and that's me—are only kids once. So I'm gonna be a kid. I'm gonna play the game; I'm gonna play for Williams; and I'm gonna pass off to Dweeb—who, by the way, can handle the ball under pressure. Oh, yeah, *(picks up duffel bag)* and I'm gonna play by the rules. Now I know they ain't your rules, but they're rules. Good rules. And the rules say I gotta be on the floor in 30 minutes, so see ya later, OLD Man.

(With his foot, Phil shoves the last empty case across the floor toward Sam. Phil starts to leave.)

Sam: *(winces as the case bangs against his leg, but he quickly picks it up as he calls after Phil)* You and the other children put on your play clothes now and have fun . . . wastin' MY money!

Phil: *(turns back to Sam)* Will do, Sam, will do. But hey, look!

Sam: What?

Phil: *(pointing where the case hit Sam's leg)* Down there. Your left cuff. You spilled milk—on your LO-O-ONG pants!

(Phil walks out laughing as Sam slams the case on the cart and turns to wheel it off.) ✆

The dialogue continues to build in intensity until Phil finally walks out and Sam gets back to work.

Professional Model

In the following professional dialogue of ideas, the writer discusses the issue of players' rights in college basketball. Note that the setting for the discussion is established before the actual dialogue begins. (The following article is reprinted courtesy of *Sports Illustrated* from the November 23, 1992, issue. Copyright © 1992, Time Inc. "Players Have Rights, Too" by Phil Taylor. All rights reserved.)

Players Have Rights, Too

In a fanciful locker room showdown, college athletes go to extremes to get their due from the NCAA.

Scene: an NCAA Final Four in the not-too-distant future. It's past tip-off time for the first semifinal game, but the players have refused to take the floor. We now switch to one of the locker rooms, where a team captain is engaged in a heated conversation with an NCAA official.

Player: We're not going out there until we talk about rights.

NCAA: Rights? Good subject. CBS is paying $143 million a year for the rights to televise this NCAA tournament, so if you fellows will kindly take the floor. . . .

Player: No. I'm talking about our rights as athletes or, more accurately, our lack of rights. This has been building up for years, this feeling players have that we're almost an afterthought in the big business of college sports.

NCAA: Nonsense. You guys are the reason we're all here.

Player: Precisely. But we're not always treated that way. For instance, nearly every pencil pusher from the NCAA and its member conferences is at the Final Four, partying and having a great time. But do you know who's not here? My parents and the parents of a lot of players like me, that's who, people who can't afford the plane fares and hotel expenses. At the 1992 Final Four in Minneapolis, two Cincinnati players didn't have a single relative in the crowd. Why is it that the NCAA, which makes that $143 million you mentioned in TV rights plus a lot of other income from the tournament, won't pay to bring two family members of each player on the Final Four teams to the tournament? What would it cost? About the same as one party for reporters, coaches, college administrators, and all the other people whose livelihoods depend on the players?

NCAA: We'll appoint a committee to consider it, OK? Now, can we get started? The CBS announcers can't stall much longer. How long can the nation watch Billy Packer and Jim Nantz play H-O-R-S-E, for crying out loud? It's getting ugly.

Player: We're not finished.

NCAA: Why do we have to talk about this now?

Player: Because this is the only time we can be sure you'll listen to us. Players' grievances tend to be ignored by the NCAA because we're temporary, replaceable parts. More often than not, we keep our complaints to ourselves, figuring, Why should we start fights we won't be around to finish? The only power we have is the power not to play.

Two unnamed individuals—one who represents the authority of the NCAA and one who represents the collegiate basketball players—are the speakers in this dialogue.

The authority figure (NCAA) seems to have control during the first part of the dialogue.

NCAA: All right, go on. But speed it up.

Player: Let's talk about the transfer rules. When I signed with this school, I was under the impression that I would be playing for the coach who recruited me. But before I even enrolled, he left for another job—the way Rollie Massimino did when he left Villanova for UNLV in 1992. There's nothing wrong with a coach's leaving one job for another, but if I want to change schools, I have to sit out a year. How fair is that?

NCAA: The rule is there so a player won't jump from school to school on a whim.

Player: But a school can take away a player's scholarship on little more than a whim. A lot of fans don't know that athletic scholarships are renewed every year. All the leverage belongs to the school—to the coach, actually. Worse, in order to leave a Division I school and go on scholarship at another, a player has to be released from his scholarship at his original school. That's usually a formality, but not always. When Lawrence Funderburke wanted to transfer from Indiana in 1990, Bob Knight wouldn't release him from his scholarship unless he approved Funderburke's choice of a new school. A coach shouldn't have that right.

NCAA: You talk about rights, but what about privileges? A player gets the chance to travel throughout the U.S., all expenses paid. He makes contacts that will help him in the future. Above all, he gets a free education. Do you know how many students would give their right arms to have that chance?

Player: It's not as though the players give nothing in return. As for the education, we've been taught to think clearly enough to realize when we're getting a raw deal.

NCAA: Listen. Can you hear the crowd out there? It's clamoring for you guys. Don't the fans have a right to see the game they paid for?

Player: Good point. The fans pay to see us play, and the networks pay a fortune to show our games. This is a billion-dollar industry, and without us it wouldn't exist. College sports is the only hugely successful enterprise I know of in this country in which the workers don't get paychecks.

NCAA: What do you want?

Player: In addition to doing what I've already mentioned, change the rules so that players can have a modest income from basketball-related sources. If a coach can make a small fortune from a sneaker company for having his players wear a certain brand of shoe, why can't we get a piece of the action? Why should the NCAA be able to turn the bloodhounds loose when it hears that a magazine might pay Christian Laettner a few bucks for keeping a diary of his senior season with Duke?

NCAA: I'll bring it up at the next NCAA convention. Now will you play?

Player: Sure, all four teams have agreed to play down at the park—shirts and skins. The winner is the national champion. Everyone's invited.

NCAA: What about tonight's game? What about TV?

Player: Tell Packer and Nantz to keep playing H-O-R-S-E.

NCAA: Wait. You can't just . . . I mean, you have no right. . . .

Player: That's what we've been trying to tell you. ✐

Many important points on both sides of the players' rights issue are debated throughout the dialogue.

By the end of the debate, control seems to be in the hands of the "upstarts," the young basketball players.

"Thomas Black Bull
Learns how to cope alone
And enters a new world;
The life of a bronco rider."   —Hugo Hwang

Response to Reading

One of the best ways to respond to a piece of
literature is to write about it on a very personal
level—in a series of journal entries, in a letter to
the author, in an imaginary conversation with
one of the characters, and so on. Writing helps
readers to put their thoughts about a text at arm's
length where they can be explored from a number
of different angles.

Read and React

<u>Discussion:</u> Write a thoughtful personal response to a book, poem, play, or short story. Your response may be a letter to the author or to one of the characters, a journal entry (or entries) focusing on a certain part of your reading, an imaginary dialogue with one of the characters, a poem expressing a specific thought or feeling about the text, or an essay (paragraph) exploring your personal connection to your reading. Review the model responses that follow for ideas for your writing. Then refer to the basic guidelines below to help you develop your work.

Searching and Selecting

1. **Selecting** • Choose a piece of literature that you have recently read on your own or as part of your classroom work. (To write an effective response, you must know the text well and have a genuine personal interest in it.)

2. **Reading** • Or read a new book, short story, or poem for this activity. Ask your teacher and classmates for their recommendations.

Generating the Text

3. **Collecting** • Generate some initial thoughts and feelings about your subject through exploratory free writing. (Use the questions listed on the "Responding to Literature" activity sheet as starting points for your writing.)

4. **Reviewing** • Review your free writing for ideas for your personal-response paper. Perhaps you identified some thoughts and feelings you would like to share in a letter to the author. Or maybe you identified some personal connections between the text and your own life. You could explore these connections in a personal essay. Then again, an idea for a poem might have developed in your exploratory writing. (The point is to think and write and explore until a specific idea for your work starts to take shape.)

Writing and Revising

5. **Writing** • Develop the first draft of your response freely and naturally as thoughts come to mind—or according to any planning or organizing you may have done.

6. **Revising** • Carefully review your first draft, first for the overall flow of your ideas, and then for the effectiveness of the individual parts (paragraphs, sentences, and words). Have a classmate review your work as well. Revise and refine accordingly.

Evaluating

Does the writing clearly communicate a thoughtful response to a piece of literature?

Has proper attention been given to accuracy and detail?

Does the writing form a meaningful whole, moving smoothly and clearly from beginning to end?

Responding to Literature

Use the questions that follow to help you explore your thoughts and feelings about the pieces of literature you read. This list is not meant to cover all the issues that might concern you, and it should be used only as a starting point for exploratory writing or journal responses. Your own thoughts and feelings are always your best resource when responding to literature.

1. What were your feelings after reading the opening chapter(s) of this book? After reading half of the book? After finishing the book?

2. Did this book make you laugh? Cry? Cringe? Smile? Cheer? Explode? Explain your reaction.

3. What connections are there between the book and your own life? Explain.

4. What are the best parts of this book? Why? What are the worst parts of this book? Why?

5. What is the author saying about life and living through this book? Explain.

6. What parts of the book seem most believable? Why? What parts seem unbelievable? Why?

7. Do you like the ending of the book? Why or why not? Do you think there is more to tell? What do you think might happen next?

8. What do you feel is the most important word in the book? The most important passage? The most important element (an event, a character, a feeling, a place, a decision)? Why is it important?

9. In what ways are you like any of the characters? Explain.

10. Do any of the characters remind you of friends, family members, or classmates? Explain.

11. What character would you like to be in this book? Why? What personality traits of this character would you like to acquire? Explain.

12. What would you and your favorite character talk about in your first conversation? Begin the conversation.

13. Do you think the title fits the book? Why or why not?

14. What makes you wonder in this book? Why? What confuses you in this book? Why?

15. What came as a surprise in the book? Why?

16. Has this book helped you in any way? Explain.

17. How have you changed after reading this book? Explain.

18. How do you picture the author of this book? Why do you picture him or her in this way?

19. What questions would you like answered after reading this book?

20. Who else should read this book? Why? Who shouldn't read this book? Why?

Student Model

In this essay, student writer Holly Morrell explores the following question: What if Buck, the canine hero in *Call of the Wild*, had not been so tough? You will notice that the writer asks this question after an effective portrayal of the real Buck.

The first paragraph presents Buck in action as a lead sled dog.

In the second part of the essay, the writer describes what would probably have happened to Buck if he hadn't been so strong.

Buck

Buck strained in the leather harness, lean muscles taut in the effort to pull the sled. He could sense a tightening of the traces as his sled mates struggled in unison. Up the snow-covered slope they went, breath showing as frequent puffs of white like the lacy bits of cloud that decorated the sharp blue sky. Buck, the lead dog, could feel ice caking uncomfortably between his frosty paws, but he still tugged, grunting with the effort. No way would he let frozen paws stop him now, not with only a few yards to go before they would crest the hill and slide easily down the other side. He could not let his life of toil get to him now after learning how to survive in the hostile Alaskan environment.

Buck, as portrayed in Jack London's *Call of the Wild*, was the hard worker described above. But, what if Buck hadn't been a fighter? What if he had lacked the will to survive?

If Buck were passive, the other sled dogs would have stolen his food out from under his nose, taking advantage of his dainty, slow eating habits developed by a past life of luxury. Eventually, not willing to defend himself, he would have weakened as a result of lack of food and too much work. He would have ignored the insistent nips and snarls of Dave, the wheeler dog. Withdrawing into himself, Buck would have tried to escape reality and would have longed for his previous style of living in California.

Spitz would have beaten Buck up a lot and then finally ignored him, not thinking him worth the while. The dramatic fight between Buck and Spitz would have most likely not occurred. The passive Buck would not have had the personality to hate Spitz, and Spitz wouldn't have perceived him as a threat.

Buck would have succumbed to the "survival of the fittest" and would have died, leaving an opening for another stronger dog to take his place. The passive Buck cannot be compared to the hard-working dog we know. ✍

Student Model

In this model, student writer Hugo Hwang responds in a free-verse poem to Thomas Black Bull, the main character in *When the Legends Die*. Note that the poem captures Thomas's struggle to hold on to his Indian heritage. (This poem first appeared in the June 1992 commemorative issue of *High School Writer*. It is reprinted with permission.)

Poetry provides an effective way to express a deeply felt emotion or belief.

When the Legends Die

Wanting to be free like his ancestors,
But in the white man's world.
Even now betrayed by his people.
Now, he is alone and empty.

Thomas Black Bull
Learns how to cope alone
And enters a new world;
The life of a bronco rider.
But even this does not
Give him everlasting happiness.
Never will it.
Eventually, dreams form,
Making him slowly think about his past.

When the legends die,
The dream is over.
Nothing can ever change him,
A Ute Indian,
Keeping his own legend alive.

Student Model

In this letter to author Maya Angelou, student writer Kate Keefe shares her thoughts and feelings about Ms. Angelou's book *All God's Children Need Traveling Shoes.* Note that Ms. Keefe makes many personal connections between the book and her own life.

Madbury, New Hampshire
September 30, 1992

Ms. Maya Angelou
Ghana, Africa

Dear Ms. Angelou,

After I had read *I Know Why the Caged Bird Sings*, I was very anxious to read *All God's Children Need Traveling Shoes* because your first book left me wondering about how your life and your son's life continued to be.

The writer explains her motive for reading *All God's Children.*

The reason that *All God's Children Need Traveling Shoes* appealed to me was because in social studies I have studied about black civil rights, and so many of the people that you mention in your book were familiar and of interest to me. Although I think that probably your book appeals mostly to an older age group because a lot of people my age still don't know much about this time in history, it was worthwhile reading for me because it made me aware that the black civil rights movement in the United States was not something that was only affecting our country, but was a worldwide situation. While sit-ins and protests were going on in America, I now know that the same kinds of things were taking place in Africa. It made me realize that no matter where you go, you can't escape being yourself. Didn't you find this to be true? It seemed to me that your going to Africa was an escape that didn't work, and that you met some of the same prejudices there that were here in America.

Throughout the letter, Ms. Keefe speaks honestly and directly with Ms. Angelou.

There was one thing that I was confused about, Ms. Angelou. You did not want blacks to be treated unjustly, and yet you treated Kojo, your "small boy," unjustly until you found out that his parents were wealthy. I had a hard time understanding this. Or, maybe I just misunderstood.

The writer parallels her search for identity with Ms. Angelou's.

But mostly, Ms. Angelou, your book taught me the importance of pride in yourself—even when life is not easy. I understand much better now what black pride is, and how important returning to Africa was in your search for yourself, because really, we are all searching for ourselves. Your book's ending showed me the journey that blacks must travel. When I read: "Despite the murders, rapes, and suicides, we have survived. The middle passage and the auction blocks have not erased us. Not humiliation, nor lynchings, individual cruelties, nor collective oppression has been able to eradicate us from the earth. We have come through despite our own ignorance and gullibility, and the ignorance and rapacious greed of our assailants." When I read those words, I could understand not only your struggle, but also my own struggle to be what I want to be. Your words help me to see, feel, hope, and dream.

Sincerely,
Kate Keefe

Student Model

In this response paper, writer Travis Taylor creates an imaginary conversation between himself and Archie Costello from *The Chocolate War* by Robert Cormier. Through this conversation, the writer attempts to understand Archie's disturbing actions.

Dialogue with Archie Costello

Me: I don't think anyone who knows you, likes you at all. Doesn't that bother you?

Archie: Not particularly. Why should it?

Me: Well, don't you like anybody?

Archie: Oddly enough I think I could have liked Jerry Renault.

Me: How could you have liked him? You did everything you could to destroy the kid.

Archie: I said that I could have liked him, not that I did like him.

Me: Could you explain that?

Archie: I probably could, but you probably wouldn't even begin to understand.

Me: Try me.

Archie: Okay. You see, I wanted Jerry to beat me, but I knew he couldn't. But there was always that little chance, you see?

Me: No.

Archie: Well, I told you, you wouldn't understand.

Me: Now let me get this straight. You could have liked Jerry, but you didn't because you beat him and wound up controlling almost the whole school afterward.

Archie: Basically, yes.

Me: Okay, I'll bite. Why?

Archie: Because if Jerry had beaten me, then he would have proved I'm wrong. I mean everybody is so predictable. Everybody wants their little bit of power. The teachers want power over the students. The upperclassmen want power over the underclassmen. Parents want power over their kids. Everyone wants a little power, so they can forget that they don't really have any power at all. I thought Jerry might be different, because he wasn't interested in power. And that was how he might have won. But since he didn't want to fall in line and play the power game, everybody jumped on his head. All I had to do was set things up and give the kids and Brother Leon a chance to do what they already wanted to do anyhow—squash Jerry. So, he just got taken out of the game. And now he'll be just like everyone else. Or else he'll stay on the sidelines. Either way it doesn't matter. I won.

Me: Yeah, I guess that's what I was afraid of. ✐

Note that the conversation is written in script form, much like a scene from a play.

Archie's explanation provides an effective self-analysis of his actions.

Professional Model

Professional writer Anne-Marie Oomen has a special interest in women writers, especially regional women writers interested in sharing and preserving the stories of local people. In the model that follows, which happens to be an excerpt from a journal entry, Ms. Oomen makes a personal connection to something she read about storytelling in a nonfiction book entitled *Woman, Native, Other* (Indiana University Press, 1989) by Trinh T. Minh-Ha.

Hidden Storytellers

Ms. Oomen's personal reaction to the first chapter is immediately established.

In the first chapter of her book, when Trinh T. Minh-Ha talks about the many hidden storytellers in today's world—people who are uninterested in sharing stories from their past—I couldn't help but think of my own parents.

A specific storytelling situation is described to prove a point.

Whenever I would ask my mother to tell me stories of her life, she seldom offered me any details. "Growing up in the Depression was hard." "All we did was work on the farm." But I knew the stories were there. I just had to get my mother to share them. Eventually I found a way by purposely stretching the truth so she would have to set me straight.

I would say something like, "Oh, Aunt Stella ALWAYS wore a wig." That would get my mother started. "She never wore a wig until the very end of her life when she was sick from the cancer. Don't you know. She sent Uncle Albert out, and it took him forever to find one she liked. See?"

To my mother, stories were folk tales, Disney fairy tales, or Bible stories. She thought stories were just for children, or to teach a lesson. It was just as difficult to get my father to talk about his past experiences.

The writer reflects upon her own parents as hidden storytellers.

Ironically they were much more likely to share stories between themselves. Sometimes my mother would string together "long threads" of stories, as Minh-Ha calls them, for my father. "Oh, John, Ethel Schaefer married John Griener back in '42, the same year my dad had the accident. She was in the same hospital when they took Dad to Ann Arbor. They lost their first child but then Hank came, and he married Gladys in '59, and that is who you talked to today at the Farm Bureau."

My parents had many wonderful and important stories to tell, but they simply did not consider them worth telling. There is a basic lack of personal pride in this attitude, but I continue to seek out my mother's hidden stories. I enjoy them, and as Minh-Ha encourages, I will try not to forget them. . . . ☙

"I get into the shower. The phone rings. I drip my way to the phone. The caller has hung up." —Ken Taylor

Pet Peeve

In a pet peeve, a writer reacts, humorously or sensibly, to a common, everyday annoyance. The pet peeve has become a popular personal essay form featured in many newspapers and magazines.

"That is the most annoying thing . . ."

Discussion: Write a brief personal essay about one of your pet peeves, one of those little everyday occurrences that bugs you, upsets you, frustrates you. Maybe a button on a shirt or blouse always seems to fall off when you are in a hurry, or your deodorant never works when it is supposed to, or people always seem to push or cut ahead of you when you are waiting in line. Remember to share specific examples and/or details about your pet peeve. This will best show why the behavior or situation affects you as it does. Reading the guidelines below as well as the models that follow will help you develop your writing.

Searching and Selecting

1. **Searching** • The subject of your essay can be a behavior or situation that really "sets your teeth on edge" or something that is only mildly annoying—just irritating enough to be memorable. Review your basic daily occurrences for ideas.

2. **Collecting** • If you have problems finding a subject, try making a "situations chart." Label it with headings like "at the movies," "in the cafeteria," "at the mall," "on the bus," etc. Then review these situations to see if any pet peeves emerge.

Generating the Text

3. **Noting** • Once you have a particular subject in mind, take note of your specific thoughts and feelings toward it. Ask yourself what specific experience(s) comes to mind when you think of this subject, what exactly causes your negative reaction, why you react the way you do, what you have done to remedy this annoyance, and so on.

4. **Shaping** • Think about how you want to organize or develop your pet peeve. For example, you might want to focus on one specific experience in your writing, or you might decide to discuss the subject in more general terms. Also, consider the tone you intend to use. Are you going to be serious, playful, or sarcastic? The choice is yours.

Writing and Revising

5. **Writing** • Now write your first draft . . . either according to the organization you've planned, or more freely, filling in with details and ideas as they occur to you.

6. **Reviewing** • Read over your draft several times (both silently and aloud), making sure your essay is organized, clear, and consistent in tone. Revise and refine your pet peeve until it says exactly what you want it to say.

Evaluating

Does the essay focus on an identifiable pet peeve?

Is it made clear why the situation or behavior is annoying?

Is the essay organized, clear, and smoothly written?

Will readers appreciate the treatment of the subject?

Student Model

This student essay details the frustration involved in trying to accomplish a basic task under pressure. The writer, Chris Hirsig, clearly illustrates how being late for work makes the task impossible to complete. Happily, an alternative solution is discovered that does not involve a "stitch in time."

Button, Button, Who's Got the Button?

Sharing details of time and place increases the urgency of a minor problem.

Darn it! There goes a button, and you're already fourteen minutes late for work. Why does a button hang in there month after month and then at the most inconvenient time let loose? And why is it that when the button falls to the floor, it always rolls under the dresser where it blends in perfectly with the carpet?

Each step in the repair process seems to create new difficulties.

After retrieving the button, the search begins for a needle and thread. As you might expect, the needle and thread are never where they should be, especially now that you're in a hurry. Finally, you locate the sewing tin and begin to pry it open. A stubbed fingernail or two later, you are ready to go. So, with a needle in one hand and the wrong-colored thread in the other, you begin to attempt the impossible—getting that tiny piece of thread through an even tinier hole in the needle. After several awkward attempts, you decide that the only way you're going to thread this needle is to use a larger needle.

The narrator seizes upon a different approach to the problem.

You feel pretty smart when the thread passes through the new needle on the first try. Such a simple solution! You knot the thread, hold the button in place, and insert the needle into the back of the first hole. You begin to pull the needle through, but for some reason it stops. You pull again—harder. You pick up the shirt, turn it inside out, and examine the back of the button. You can't help but moan out loud. But then, how could you have known the larger needle was too thick to pass through the hole in the button? So much for simple solutions.

Still, a solution is near . . . in this case, as near as the closet door. You open the door, grab the first shirt you see, quickly inspect the buttons for durability, and swing your arm through the sleeve. Who says you have to know how to sew on a button to survive in today's world? ☯

Student Model

In this model, student writer Ben Hawkinson expresses his feelings toward the traditional potluck church dinner. There is a negative tone at the beginning of the essay. However, that tone changes little by little as the writing develops.

Potluck

The opening paragraph quickly establishes the humorous tone of this essay.

Circa October, 1991. I was sitting in church reading the bulletin. I greeted people who walked by; I was happy. The Bears were going to play, I had no homework, and there was no communion (shorter service). I was reading the back of the bulletin for our church's fast facts. Dorcas Circle was meeting Tuesday, Mr. Meyers was usher—then I saw it. "We're going to hold our annual autumn POTLUCK." This one word held more fear and panic in my soul than the devil himself. Ever since old Pastor Bill was in our church, I've remembered these . . . these potlucks. I started to reminisce, recall, and remember.

There are three ways to learn of a potluck: read the bulletin, notice the sign-up chart, or hear from Emma "someone's been baking" Gustavson. She was an older member who lived for church potlucks. Her greatest aspiration was to know what everyone was bringing. She didn't bother to read the sign-up sheet; that was too easy.

The sign-up sheet. I believe the problem with potlucks starts here. Instead of listing chicken dishes, molds and jellies, and casseroles, they should just list "Food that people enjoy."

The author focuses on a staple of potluck suppers—the casserole.

The casserole: "baking dish in which food is cooked and served." This definition is the basis and foundation of any church potluck. There are many types of casseroles: chicken, beef, tuna, and "special." I must admit that I like one type of casserole. The one with chicken, a gray substance, and crushed Jays on top. It's strange, but it appeals to me. A casserole must always be in a casserole dish. There's the basic white from the '60s and early '70s with light blue flowers on the sides, or the clear dishes which sit in straw containers. My mom has both.

By the end of the essay, the writer reveals his true feelings about potlucks.

Other Bay potluck culinary examples include rolled ham, Ruth Hill's dill pickles, deviled eggs, rolls, mushy butter, vegetable Jell-O molds, and some savior always brings ham sandwiches. To drink, there is the infamous "Church Kool-Aid." This is an elderly woman's rendition of what she thinks Kool-Aid should taste like. It's like colored sugar water with no fruit taste.

When you're finally done going through the line, your plate has molded into one entree. A chunky (chicken), red (Jell-O), soggy (bread), smelly (eggs) mush. Delicious. . . .

Professional Model

While writer and teacher Ken Taylor never says it directly, the tone of this pet peeve strongly implies that the author would be happy with a return to a simpler mode of communication. The essay summarizes the writer's ongoing (and unequal) battle with telephones of assorted sizes and shapes, a war being waged on a variety of fronts.

The opening lines describe a series of frustrating incidents involving the telephone.

The listing of incidents implies the author's war with telephones is ongoing.

The suggested solution shows that the writer sees no real answer to his problem.

Telephone Tyranny

I get into the shower. The phone rings. I drip my way to the phone. The caller has hung up. I have an urgent call to make and hurry to a pay phone on the corner. The phone is out of order. I try a half dozen phones. They are all inoperable. After I find a phone with a dial tone, it eats my only quarter and I dial the wrong number. The phone rings on my nightstand at 4:00 a.m. I jump a good three feet, and knock the lamp off the stand on my way back to earth. A voice I never heard before wants to know if Harry is there. I don't know any Harrys.

I'm on the parkway going 65 miles an hour. I look in the rearview mirror. There's a car about to drive right through me. The driver is talking on his cellular car phone. I'm in the middle of eating dinner. The phone rings. I answer the phone. There's a recorded voice on the phone wanting to know if I'm happy with my present insurance coverage. I return to my food. The phone rings again. This time it's someone from the phone company who wants to sell me "call-waiting."

I can hear the phone ringing as I get off the elevator for my apartment. The phone keeps on ringing. I fumble for my keys, open the door, rush to the phone, and the caller has hung up. (Probably the same person who calls when I'm in the shower.)

I get an answering machine. When I get home there are six calls on the machine. I push "play" and get to listen to six dial tones after the callers have hung up without saying anything.

I call a friend at his office. A secretary tells me I can call him direct on a different extension. Would I like to hang up and make the call again? No, I wouldn't. Okay, she will "try" to transfer my call. She tries. The next thing I hear is a dial tone.

I call a friend at home. She asks me if I'd mind holding. She has another call "coming in." I call another friend at his office. He sounds as if he were talking from the moon. He says he's using his new "speaker phone" and isn't it great?

I'm seriously thinking of taking up letter writing. ✎

Academic Writing

"Organically grown cotton duds present one new planet—protecting option." —Michelle Kearns

Essay of Information

An essay of information presents the important facts and details related to a specific subject. The writer's challenge in this form of writing is to organize the information so it speaks clearly and effectively to readers.

Getting Your Facts Straight

Discussion: Write an informational essay based on a list of facts you have collected about a subject of personal interest. (Refer to two different sources of information—reference books and/or magazines—for your facts.) Or use either of the two prepared "facts sheets" (pp. 107-108) as a starting point for your work. All of the facts you include in your essay should support a main idea about your subject. Make sure that your writing reads smoothly and clearly from the introductory paragraph to your closing thought. Refer to the model essays that follow and the guidelines below to help you with your writing.

Searching and Selecting

1. **Searching** • Think of a subject you would like to know more about—a subject related to your work in a particular class or to one of your other interests. Page through your textbooks for possible subjects, or brainstorm for ideas with a group of classmates.

2. **Selecting** • Focus your attention on subjects that have been thoroughly discussed in various texts since you will want a rich resource of facts to work with in your essay. (If you can't find a suitable subject, remember that you can use one of the prepared facts sheets.)

Generating the Text

3. **Collecting** • Don't worry about the order of the facts and details that you collect. Simply list important pieces of information as you come across them. Use your own words as much as possible when recording information. (See how it was done on one of the facts sheets.)

4. **Planning** • Review your facts sheet, looking for a main idea or impression about your subject that could serve as a focus for your writing. Then circle or underline those facts and details in your list that support this focus. Also decide how these supporting details could be developed into separate paragraphs in your essay. You might find it helpful to organize these details in an outline.

Writing and Revising

5. **Writing** • Develop your first draft according to your planning and organizing. Devote some extra time and effort to the opening paragraph. It should engage your readers' interest and make them want to read on.

6. **Revising** • Carefully review your first draft, making sure it flows smoothly and clearly from one paragraph to the next. Then focus your attention on the specific thoughts and details in each individual paragraph. Revise and refine accordingly.

Evaluating

Is the essay clearly focused and organized?

Does it contain effective supporting detail?

Will readers appreciate the treatment of the subject?

Student Model

Student writer Hillary Bachman wrote this essay of information about humpback whales after going on a whale watch. She saw humpback whales *breaching*, *flipper slapping*, and *feeding* at close range. Some of the facts in her essay are based on her own firsthand experiences; other facts come from two reference books. A "facts sheet" follows her essay.

Humpback Whales:
Graceful Giants of the Deep

The author introduces the topic with some interesting facts.

Humpback whales may be the slowest of all of the whales, but they are, by far, the most playful and amazing species. One of their many playful acts is breaching, the act of lifting their bodies (40 tons of body mass extended over a 50-foot frame when fully grown) almost completely out of the water. They also enjoy slapping their huge white flippers against the water, a sound which can be heard from great distances. In addition, they will thrust their flukes (the tail portion of their bodies) straight out of the water. Since humpbacks are drawn to ships, it is very easy to see them perform these tricks on whale watches.

Many whales have been known to "sing," but the most wonderful singers are the humpbacks. One of their songs may last from 7 to 30 minutes before it is repeated. The singer will float straight up and down with its head pointed toward the ocean floor. One man who records the songs of humpbacks said, "In the early evening there were only a few sounds, but soon one whale after another joined in, almost as if they were tuning [up]. Later, it seemed like one group of whales would sing one verse and another group would sing another verse." No one knows for sure why the whales sing, but one theory suggests that it is a means of communicating, a way to find other whales; another theory suggests that they sing simply for the sheer joy of making noise.

Note that each paragraph deals with a related set of facts and details.

With all of their body mass and blubber, you would think that whales could remain in cold water year-round. But this is not true. Humpbacks, like other whales, must migrate. Some humpbacks begin their journey in October. These whales are generally mature females accompanied by their yearling calves. The next to go are the immature males and females. Last, but not least, are the pregnant females and the bulls. These journeys, which can be over 2,000 miles long, usually take about two months. The fat layer beneath the whale's skin is a food reserve on migrations.

It's hard to say how the whales find their way to their destinations. They may rely on their excellent sense of hearing to pick up low-frequency sound waves which bounce off familiar ocean topography. Scientists also believe that they may look for familiar landforms. Two researchers recently detected a magnetic material, probably magnetite, in humpbacks, which may allow them to migrate by sensing the earth's magnetic field. This has led other researchers to think that whales get stranded because they are drawn to coasts with low magnetic intensities. This would also explain how they could follow such precise migration paths.

It may seem impossible that such large animals can be so affectionate and caring, but they really are, especially when it comes to their mates. They enjoy brushing up against each other and patting each other with their huge white flippers. Sometimes a bull will escort the young when they migrate north again, and will help protect and raise them.

A calf (generally one per female) is born in a lagoon or harbored area to protect it from crashing waves and killer whales. If the calf starts to sink, that is a sign that it must be pushed to the surface by the cow (mature female whale) for air. Soon after birth, it begins feeding. A calf consumes up to two gallons of milk at each feeding, and it may feed 48 times a day. It's understandable that calves grow as much as 200 pounds a day and are 50 feet long by the age of one. The cows generally take care of their calves for their first six to twelve months of life.

Humpback whales eat very tiny creatures called plankton and krill. Krill are little shrimplike creatures which the humpback eats by making a circle of bubbles around the krill, engulfing them, and then swimming up to the surface with its mouth wide open, a process called gulping. They halfway close their mouths, pushing the excess water out through a "built-in strainer" called the baleen, which is made out of the same material that hair is. A whale can gulp one to two tons of krill at a time.

Since prehistoric times, people have killed whales for meat, oil, and fertilizer. Humpback whales have been hunted especially heavily because of their prized whale oil. Since there were no "bag limits," as many as 23 humpback whales could be killed by a single gunner in one day. Whales are still being killed today by certain Eskimo people, not as drastically as 15 years ago, but even so, their numbers are diminishing at an alarming rate.

It would be a shame to lose these amazing creatures. They are gentle and very affectionate. We don't want the humpbacks' mysterious song to be a thing of the past. But we can't turn to zoos when the humpbacks' numbers shrink to a precious few, like we did with the California condor or the bald eagle, because it would take too much space, time, food, and money to keep a captive humpback healthy and happy. So we must protect the humpbacks' natural habitat and think of its future as a free and wild creature. ✍

Throughout the essay, several aspects of whale behavior are identified.

The author hopes that readers will share her enthusiasm for the humpback whales.

Facts Sheet

Humpback Whales

1 are called bulls, cows, and calves
2 give birth to live young in lagoons protected from surf and killer whales
3 drink milk from the mother's body—up to two gallons per feeding—48 feedings per day
4 grow up to 200 pounds a day, reach 50 feet long at one year
5 usually have only one calf at a time and stay with it for at least a year
6 after birth must be helped to the surface for air by their mothers
7 spend summers feeding in cool northern waters
8 make two-month long, 2,000-mile migrations beginning in October
(first females with young, then young adults, then pregnant females and bulls)
9 migrate to warm tropical waters for the birth of young
10 Bulls sometimes escort the migration back north and help raise the young.
11 are affectionate mates, brushing and patting each other with their flippers
12 have life spans ranging from 15 to 60 years
13 have been killed by people for meat, oil, fertilizer, etc., since prehistoric times
14 are still hunted (numbers are down from 102,000 to 8,700)
15 can lift their 40 tons up to 52 feet in the air
16 are the most playful species of whale
17 have unique white flippers that are one-third the length of their bodies
18 can carry up to half a ton of barnacles (marine crustaceans)
19 swim slowly and often thrash their tails (called *flukes*) out of the water
20 make impressive leaps from the water called *breaching*
21 frequently travel in groups called *schools* or *herds*
22 have a fat layer beneath their skin, *blubber*, a food reserve on migrations
23 have lighter-than-water blubber that increases their buoyancy
24 are *floaters* (float when they die)
25 breathe through two nostrils called *blowholes*, exhaling water vapor (a spout)
26 are *baleen* whales, and have no teeth
27 strain the water through baleen sieves (a material like human hair)
28 eat tiny *plankton* (plants and animals) or *krill* (shrimplike animals)
29 can gulp one to two tons of krill at once
30 can't smell, taste, or see well, but have excellent hearing
31 use sonar—bouncing sound waves off surfaces and ocean topography
32 may use low-frequency sound waves to find their way on migration
33 Certain researchers think magnetite in whales helps them navigate.
34 Others think precise migration paths relate to magnetism.
35 may get stranded when drawn to coasts with low magnetic intensities
36 sing songs consisting of series of sounds lasting 7 to 30 minutes
37 sing to communicate with and find other whales or just for "fun"
38 A man recording humpbacks said, "In the early evening there were only a few sounds, but soon one whale after another joined in, almost as if they were tuning. Later, it seemed like one group of whales would sing one verse and another group would sing another verse."

Professional Model

In this essay, Michelle Kearns provides a great deal of information about new, environmentally correct clothing. A "facts sheet" follows her essay. (This article by Michelle Kearns first appeared in OMNI, June 1992. It is reprinted by permission of OMNI, © 1992, OMNI Publications International, Ltd.)

Natural Collection:
**Thanks to the ecouture movement,
the human race may not go out of fashion.**

At first, environmental clothing might sound boring. However, hiking boots made from diapers capture the reader's attention.

Sawdust, metal shavings, disposable diapers, coffee filters, foam rubber—garbage? Nope. Put these common, everyday landfill items together and you make the latest in environmentally correct apparel: hiking shoes.

"We're recycling things that won't biodegrade," says Scott Taylor, vice president of Deja Inc., the Portland-based company responsible for the sporty Deja shoe. "We take the trim waste from disposable diapers, reprocess it into a new yarn, and weave it into shoe fabric." The company, whose footwear debuts nationwide next year, joins a new breed of clothing manufacturers dedicated to the eco-ethic that garments can both look good and protect the planet.

The trend—represented in everything from T-shirts and jeans to top designer collections—couldn't come at a better time. As it turns out, even apparently benign clothing isn't as environment-loving as it appears. Take a "100-percent" natural cotton shirt. Most cotton threads begin as plants nursed with generous doses of pesticides, herbicides, and defoliants. Off the farm, cotton's offenses multiply: Threads are typically washed, softened, straightened, bleached, and dyed—processes that pollute.

Organically grown cotton duds present one new planet-protecting option. And some companies are skipping as many traditional manufacturing steps as possible to save water and energy and eliminate chemical waste. The mail-order green giant, Seventh Generation, for example, touts shirts, sweaters, and sweats fashioned from unbleached, undyed, and organic cotton.

By using names and facts related to famous fashion companies, the writer gives her essay added authority.

For earth-friendly color, some eco-clothiers are turning to synthetic "bifunctional" dyes. Higgins Naturals, for example, uses the dyes to colorize polo shirts, turtlenecks, sweaters, and sweats in 20 hues, from moss green to burgundy. The dyes are slightly more expensive than the industry standard (and predictably unpopular), but the dying technique reduces the amount of water, energy, and dye waste by fixating the color completely to the fabric.

Mother Nature has also come up with her own color solution: cotton that grows in shades of brown and green. Developed by Sally Fox, who dubs her wares FoxFibre, the cotton is now woven into unisex striped T-shirts made by Esprit and in traditionally styled jeans and jackets by Levi Strauss & Co., called Naturals. The caramel-colored fabric feels like suede and doesn't fade over time like most jeans.

As green fashion sensibilities catch on with consumers, fashion experts predict American style itself may change. Bright white summer wardrobe staples could be the first casualties—most have not only been bleached, but also dyed white. "White stuff looks peculiar to me now," says Katherine Tiddens, owner of Terra Verde Trading Co., an ecological department store.

Even Georgio Armani now designs pants in unbleached, undyed linen. "It's the beginning of groundswell," confirms John Karl, chairman of the menswear department at New York's Fashion Institute of Technology. "There's going to be a retooling of the industry—more vegetable hues, fabric with nubs, and softer lines."

But eco-style also applies to fashion details. Next season's clothing lines will sport earth-friendly zippers, buttons, and even elastic. Lynda Grose, the developer of Ecollection, Esprit's new environmental line, discovered most suppliers sell belt buckles, zippers, rivets, and buttons made from rust-prone metals. To prevent oxidation, they require electroplating, another polluting process. Esprit's solution: rust-proof copper alloys.

Clothing companies are also finding fashion solutions in the jungle. The tagua tree from the rain forests of Ecuador produces an alternative to plastic buttons. Demand for the tree's ivory-like nuts, carved and sewn on shirt fronts by manufacturers such as Esprit, Smith & Hawken, and Patagonia, has created a sustainable income for locals.

Eco-fashion details are also found here at home. Recycled inner tubes are now turning up on canvas accessories. As Cameron Trotter of Used Rubber U.S.A. suggests, "Tread marks can be beautiful."

The writer includes a great deal of new information in her essay. Her carefully chosen facts keep readers interested right up to the final catchy quotation.

Facts Sheet

Natural Collection

1 landfill items for environmentally correct apparel
2 hiking boots made from garbage
3 nonbiodegradable waste like diaper trim for yarn for shoe fabric
4 Deja Inc. in Portland producing such footwear
5 100-percent natural cotton not "natural"
6 cotton plants = doses of pesticides, herbicides, defoliants
7 cotton threads washed, softened, straightened, bleached, dyed = polluting process
8 organically grown cotton planet protecting
9 Seventh Generation, mail-order clothing
10 organically grown cotton, no bleach or dye
11 Higgins Naturals' 20 bifunctional dyes, expensive, greens to burgundy
12 completely fixate color to fabric
13 Mother Nature cotton in green and brown
14 naturally colored cotton developed/grown by Sally Fox
15 calls her fabric FoxFibre
16 used for Esprit shirts and Levi Strauss & Co. jeans (Naturals)
17 caramel-colored FoxFibre feels like suede, nonfading
18 bright white style over?
19 Terra Verde Trading Co. an ecological department store
20 designer Georgio Armani, fashions of unbleached, undyed linen
21 John Karl, chair menswear department N. Y. Fashion Institute of Technology
22 predicts retooling: vegetable colors, nubby fabric, softer lines
23 fashion details, earth-friendly zippers, buttons, elastic
24 Lynda Grose, developer of Esprit's Ecollection
25 avoids rust-prone metals and polluting electrolyting processes
26 rust-proof copper alloys instead
27 fashion solutions in the jungle
28 tagua tree buttons (Ecuador rain forest)
29 Esprit, Smith & Hawken, and Patagonia using these ivory-like nut buttons
30 creates jobs for local people
31 Cameron Trotter, Used Rubber U.S.A. says, "Tread marks can be beautiful."

Additional Facts Sheet

Dancing

The following facts sheet can serve as a guide as you collect facts for a subject of your own choosing, or it can serve as a starting point for your work on an essay on dancing. Feel free to conduct your own research and add additional facts about dancing to the list.

1   the act of moving the body in rhythm (usually to music)
2   an art form telling a story, setting a mood, expressing emotions
3   a recreation offering fun, relaxation, companionship
4   shown in prehistoric paintings and sculptures 20,000 years ago
5   natural rhythmic movement in children
6   scientifically reveals things about a people's culture
7   therapy treats physical and emotional problems
8   a part of worship throughout human history
9   was used by American Indians for good weather and crops
10 provides theatrical entertainment—ballet, tap dancing, etc.
11 ballet beginnings in Italian royal courts (1400's)
12 ballet—the trunk of the body remains relatively calm
13 early ballet—based on moral or political stories
14 modern ballets—stories, or primarily response to music
15 Isadora Duncan, modern dance pioneer, movements influenced by nature
16 Duncan—barefoot, flowing clothing, no scenery
17 modern dance primarily movement for its own sake
18 modern dance—tumbling, rolling, and other acrobatics
19 *choreographers*—dance composers
20 social, part of a people's tradition (folk dance)
21 developed self-control and skill at war, according to Greek philosopher Plato
22 entertained nobility in Middle Ages
23 Renaissance King Louis XIV of France formalized ballet.
24 in the 1800's—to glorify the individual
25 new social dances from the common people
26 black tap from combining African, Irish, and English folk dances
27 chorus line cancan originating in France
28 1900's cakewalk, tango, Charleston, swing, rock 'n' roll, disco, break dancing
29 African dance essential to village-life events like birth or death
30 together, African men, women, and children (rarely alone or with partners)
31 Africans' six rhythms (head, trunk, arms, legs, each to different beats)
32 primary focus (African dance) overall natural flow of movement
33 body painting for expressiveness (African dancing)
34 Oriental dance traditions thousands of years old
35 Asian theater—dance, music, pantomime, speech, and puppetry combined
36 gives significant messages in subtle, Oriental facial and hand gestures
37 shows historical events, legends, or myths (Asian)

What else do you want or need to know about dancing to write your essay?

Additional Facts Sheet

Batteries

The following facts sheet can serve as a guide as you collect facts for a subject of your own choosing, or it can serve as a starting point for your work on an essay on batteries. Feel free to conduct your own research and add additional facts about batteries to this list.

1   produce electricity by means of chemical action
2   are a "group of connected cells"
3   consist of one or more units called electric cells
4   power start-up of automobile engines
5   supply emergency electricity in power failures
6   must be discarded after one of their chemicals is used up (primary)
7   exist in many standard sizes, from 1/20 of an ounce to nearly a ton
8   were first developed by Italian scientist Count Alessandro Volta (1790's)
9   can be rechargeable (secondary or storage)
10   have a chemical substance conducting electric current—electrolyte
11   use jellylike or pastelike electrolytes—dry cells
12   use liquid electrolytes—wet cells (some primary, most secondary)
13   have two structures called electrodes (dry, primary)
14   have a different kind of chemically active material for each electrode
15   have one electrode (anode) negatively charged due to electrolyte
16   have the other electrode (cathode) positively charged
17   are carbon-zinc cells, alkaline cells, mercury cells (major primary ones)
18   for flashlights and toys are usually all-purpose carbon-zinc
19   use a zinc-case anode in carbon-zinc batteries
20   use manganese dioxide in central carbon rod (cathode)
21   use electrolyte paste of ammonium chloride, zinc chloride, water (zinc-carbon)
22   use a thin separator (between electrode materials when battery is not in use)
23   produce electricity from zinc oxidizing (zinc-carbon)
24   use oxidation sending excess electrons in circuit from anode to carbon rod
25   die after manganese dioxide is gone (carbon-zinc)
26   use potassium hydroxide electrolyte (alkaline)
27   produce higher current, more efficient than carbon-zinc (alkaline)
28   five to eight times longer lasting than carbon-zinc (alkaline)
29   produce constant voltage with cathode of mercuric oxide (mercury)
30   good for scientific devices and hearing aids (mercury)
31   called lead-acid or nickel-cadmium (secondary)
32   use spongy lead for negative electrodes (lead-acid)
33   use lead dioxide for positive electrodes (lead-acid)
34   have an electrolyte of sulfuric acid and water (lead-acid)
35   are recharged by reversing their chemical reactions
36   used in car and truck ignitions (lead-acid)

What else might you want or need to know about batteries to write your essay?

"How does the trash get all the way from your kitchen to the dump on Staten Island?" —Laura Bruno

Essay to Explain a Process

In this type of essay, a writer explains how to do or make something or how something works. The writer's challenge is to speak clearly and carefully so that readers can easily follow the directions or explanation.

"The first thing you do . . ."

Discussion: Write an essay (paragraph) in which you explain how a process works or how to make or do something. Your goal in this paper is to speak clearly, in a helpful voice, so that readers can easily follow your explanation or directions. Provided below are basic guidelines to help you develop your writing. Also note the writing models following these guidelines. Additional information can be found in *Writers INC*. (Refer to "Writing, An explanation" in the index.)

Searching and Selecting

1. **Selecting** • You may choose to explain a more common, everyday procedure, or you may select a process you either want to learn more about or have studied in one of your classes. Keep in mind that your subject should be of genuine interest to you and your readers. (How the HIV virus affects the immune system would be a timely, important topic. How photosynthesis works, perhaps not. How to win prizes in a radio contest, yes. How to make peanut butter cookies, well, maybe. How to stare into space, yes—if it is approached in the right way.)

2. **Reviewing** • Review your class notes or texts for ideas. Or try free-writing or clustering about your course work, noting potential subjects as they come to mind. Think of hobbies and talents you have. Brainstorm for ideas with your classmates.

Generating the Text

3. **Recording** • List related facts and details about your subject as they come to mind, or write an instant version of the finished product to see how much you already know about your subject—and how much you need to find out.

4. **Collecting** • Collect additional information and details accordingly.

5. **Organizing** • If necessary, organize the information you have collected before you write your first draft. (Generally speaking, an explanation is organized according to time—*first, second, third, meanwhile, then, finally,* etc.) Also think about the feeling or impression you want to express in your writing. (Depending on your subject, it is okay, even desirable, to put a little humor into your essay.)

Writing and Revising

6. **Writing** • Write your first draft freely, working in details and ideas according to your planning—or according to the steps in the process as you naturally know them.

7. **Revising** • Review, revise, and refine your writing before sharing it.

Evaluating

Does the explanation form a meaningful whole? Does each step lead the reader clearly and logically to the next?

Are main points supported by specific details and examples?

Will readers appreciate the treatment of this subject?

Student Model

Laura Bruno, the student writer of the essay below, presents a concise but thorough treatment of the process by which the massive amount of garbage generated each day in New York City gets from people's homes to the huge landfill on Staten Island. Each step along the "garbage trail" is explained, and the essay ends with a warning. (The article first appeared in *New Youth Connections: The Magazine Written By and For New York Youth*, September/October 1991. It is reprinted with permission.)

The topic of the essay is presented in an opening question.

The writer provides details to clarify particular phases of the process.

The writer creates a smooth sense of movement from one operation to another in the overall process.

Garbage Trail

1. How does the trash get all the way from your kitchen to the dump on Staten Island? Well, after the garbage we put out on our sidewalks is picked up by a sanitation truck, it is taken to a sorting station. The recyclable objects are taken out and sent to a recycling center, and all the rest of the garbage is loaded onto barges (boats) which carry it to the landfill.

2. The barges are covered with nets to prevent trash from spilling into the water. Near the landfill, a system of fences and nets underneath the water prevents anything that does fall in from floating out of the Fresh Kills area. There are also boats that go round picking up any garbage that gets blown into the water. Every day, between 22 and 24 barges arrive at Fresh Kills carrying 600 tons of garbage each.

3. Big, tall cranes with enormous jaws reach down, take the trash off the barges, and drop it onto trucks, which carry it uphill to the dumping site. Compactors, which look like army tanks, drive back and forth over the hill to flatten down the new garbage. Then, other trucks come and cover everything with dirt so grass can be planted.

4. The landfill is expected to be full in 12 years. When it closes, three grass-covered trash mountains will be left behind, and there won't be any place left in New York City to put all that trash. That's why we all have to start coming up with new ways to reduce, recycle, and get rid of our waste now, before it's too late. ✐

Student Model

The essay below explains a process that writer Mary Ertl has apparently thought through very carefully. (One wonders how many times she has needed to rely on this process without waking her parents.) We recommend that you imitate this clear, humorous style of writing in your own essay, but we can't recommend that you follow her advice. We are, after all, parents ourselves.

The opening lines immediately draw the reader into the essay, using the second-person "you."

Settling in for the Night

It's late. You were supposed to be home at 10:30. It is now 11:30. The lights are out and the house is silent. You tiptoe in, taking every step cautiously, knowing that at any moment your life could be in the hands of one of your unhappy parents. Are you often faced with the fear of losing life and limb while attempting to sneak in late at night? I know I've faced this problem several times; and I think it's safe to say, I have the process mastered.

One of the first things I've learned is to lubricate all outside doors. Nothing is more likely to wake your parents than the squeaking of a front or back door. They've been trained to recognize this sound several houses away. Check both doors before leaving to make sure they are still squeak-free. A second helpful hint is to clear a path from the outside doors to the stairs. If you have a house like mine, this step is the most important, because nothing is more embarrassing than stumbling over an invisible roadblock late at night. The rest of the family doesn't realize that leaving their shoes or schoolbooks in the hallway can cause a serious problem.

The transition words "first," "second," "third," etc., guide the reader through the steps of the process.

Third, I warn you about the stairs. If you do not have stairs, consider yourself lucky. Stairs present a serious challenge to the young at heart and the late. If you do have stairs, I have devised a plan and tested it with excellent results. Before you leave for the evening, walk up and down the stairs several times. In my house, every step squeaks, but certain ones squeak more loudly than the others—specifically the third, sixth, and eleventh steps. Once you find the noisy steps, always remember to skip over them. Although parents never seem to hear you when you want them to, at night they have ears like a dog, picking up every audible sound.

Now let's assume you are returning from your evening out and are ready to test the system. Before you even open the outside door, take off your shoes. (Common sense, I know, but it doesn't hurt to remind you.) Once inside the door, head immediately but carefully to the stairs. Begin your ascent, counting as you go. Again, move quickly, but carefully. If your parents think they may have heard a squeaky door or step, they will listen more carefully for another sound. One way to minimize the potential for more sounds is to outsmart your squeaky floorboards. You can do this by simply "walking" down the hallway on all fours. This distributes your weight over four limbs rather than two. Thus, your chance of causing a sound is cut in half (I think).

The last paragraph offers a final tip.

Finally, if you make it safely to your room, don't get overconfident and blow it at this late stage. Don't take time to undress. Get immediately into bed, close your eyes, and pretend to be asleep. After one of your parents checks to see if you're home—you can undress and settle in for the night.

Professional Model

In the following model, Mike Flaherty and Christina Kelly explain the proper way to prepare and enjoy mashed potatoes. The authors stir in plenty of humor by sharing comments and asides along with the steps to this recipe. (Reprinted with permission of *Sassy Magazine*, this article first appeared in the March 1992 issue. Copyright © 1992 by Sassy Publishers, Inc.)

Note that the humorous parts of this recipe are stated within parentheses. (It would seem the writers are not on a diet!)

Eat This:
Mashed Potatoes Rule, God Love 'Em

The recipe: Take 1-1/2 good-sized potatoes per person (a nutritionist would probably tell you to eat one each, but this is not about moderation; the point of mashed potatoes is to indulge yourself). Peel and cut into quarters. After you've boiled them slowly for a good 20 minutes, drain, and while still in the pot, give them a good, thorough mashing. (A word about the masher: It must be the grid kind, not the WASP-y, squiggly-line model that housewares stores try and pass off on you. Strictly for neophytes [beginners], man. Christina had a hard time finding the mighty grid masher, and Mike was the only person on staff who could sympathize.) Add a good hunk of butter (not margarine, for crying out loud!) and ample salt and pepper. Chuck in some whole milk (what are you crazy with that skim?!) till the spuds attain that not-too-stiff-not-too-runny consistency, and you're done. If you're one of those people who doesn't mind when all the foods on your plate are touching each other, you have our permission to chew your mashed potatoes and peas together, stick out your tongue and show your brother.

Professional Model

Ken Taylor, the author of this essay of explanation, appears not only to have perfected the process of avoiding homework, but has managed to turn that process into a life's work. The author's not-so-serious commentary creates a humorous manual for the nonserious student. We don't suggest you adopt the avoiding-homework process yourself, but you should enjoy reading about it. It is reprinted with permission of the author.

The Art and Practice of Avoiding Homework

The opening lines describing the subject set the essay's humorous tone.

Anyone can just not do homework. But as someone once may or may not have said, "Anything worth not doing is worth not doing well." So, you see, simply not doing something is pretty negative. However, taking active steps to avoid doing something, in this case, homework, is a whole other matter. Avoiding homework is active. You are taking positive steps to evade responsibility.

Now, the first step is to make certain you don't bring your homework assignment home with you. This doesn't mean that you don't copy the assignment off the board in all good faith, because that would just get the entire process off to a negative start. No, you have to have the homework so you can not remember to bring it home with you.

Once you leave your assignment behind, the next move is to blank your mind completely. You see, if you consciously remember you have left your homework in your locker or in your desk, then you would have to go get it. So, the thing to do is to forget all about it until you're on the bus and can't do anything about it. If you get a twinge on the bus, why naturally you can satisfy your duty by asking one of our friends who also practices the "art of homework avoidance" for the assignment, with reasonable assurance that your friend won't have it either. (You're going to need this friend later.)

The detailed explanation indicates the writer's complete understanding of the process.

As soon as you get home, immediately involve yourself in video games or television or some other activity that will occupy your mind and prevent you from contemplating homework. Don't worry because this is perfectly legitimate. After all, you've just put in a rough day at school, and you deserve a little recreation and diversion.

It's a pretty good bet that one or both of your parents are going to mention homework during dinner, probably during that little session about what you did that was interesting in school that day. At that point, you can get into serious discussion about something you dealt with that day and sidetrack any homework questions. A good technique is to pick something in history and ask them about it. (Depending on what time you eat, this history gambit can also be used to express an interest in watching the news to keep up with current events. What parent could object to their kid watching the news?)

Okay, now you have to start thinking in terms of time frames. Once you've stalled as long as you think you can, you have to figure out how much time you have to kill before you can legitimately go to bed. The tried and true initial move is to start watching a TV show or start playing a video game until you get reminded about homework. Then you can say that you just want to see the end of the show or finish the game.

Next you discover you don't have your homework assignment. So, naturally, this requires that you call someone to get the assignment. (Remember your friend on the bus?) When you call your friend, you can talk for a while because it wouldn't be polite just to call and hang up as soon as you get the assignment. And, since your friend won't have the assignment (he was just thinking about calling you), you'll have to make a couple more calls to actually get it. Stretch it out as long as you can.

When you finally do have the assignment, with any luck, it will require some special material you don't have immediately available, like file folders or some other piece of equipment. (Note: It is not okay to forget your textbook AND your homework. A missing textbook demands another set of activities entirely.) If you do require some additional material, you will either have to ask someone to take you to get it, depending where you live, or you will have to get it yourself. Either way, it will take time.

However, if you don't need anything else, you can just get on with your avoidance tactics. Announce that you are going to your room to do the assignment. Remember to keep track of the time.

In your room, it is necessary to prepare carefully to do the assignment. This means sharpening pencils, making sure you have all of the things you need to work with and that all of them are in tip-top working order. You might want to pick up your room a little because it's always good to work in an ordered and neat environment. Maybe there are a few dirty clothes that need to be taken down to the laundry room or at least put away in a hamper somewhere. Taking a shower might be a good idea as well—save you time in the morning, plus you'll feel refreshed and able to work better.

Now, if you time things right, it should be getting a little late—late enough that you might want to lie down on your bed and think about the assignment before actually getting down to doing it. At this point, you should fall asleep, and then your mother looking in will see how exhausted you were from working on your assignment.

I have only dealt with a single assignment in these suggestions. There will undoubtedly be times when you have multiple assignments. You'll be glad to know that the theory remains essentially the same no matter how many assignments you have. ◉

Each complete step toward doing homework leads to additional problems, all of which are actually part of not doing homework.

The essay ends with the promise that this process will apply to all homework situations.

Writing Workshops

Searching and Selecting

Gearing Up for Writing

This is a chance for you to take stock of your writing experiences and abilities at the beginning of the year. Consider each question carefully before answering it, and word your answers clearly and carefully. This information will make it easier for your teacher to advise you about your writing, and it will make it easier for you to evaluate your writing progress later in the year when you refer back to this survey.

1. What are the last pieces of writing you have completed? (Identify two or three.)

2. What forms of writing are you most familiar with? *(Reports, essays, paragraphs, reviews, stories, poems, essay-test answers, etc.)*

3. What is the most successful or meaningful paper you've written in the past year or two? Briefly describe it.

4. Do you usually write on subjects of your own choosing or on assigned topics? Which do you like better and why?

5. What is your greatest strength as a writer? Explain.

6. What stage in the writing process gives you the most trouble? (*Getting started, focusing my efforts, organizing, drafting, revising, editing,* etc.) Explain.

7. Do you follow a set revising strategy? What sorts of changes do you normally make when you revise?

8. What type of writing gives you the most problems? What type of writing would you like to learn more about? What specific writing skills would you like to practice?

Review this survey each quarter to see how your writing attitudes, skills, and interests change throughout the school year.

Writing is mind traveling . . .

READ: In the opening discussion of the writing process in your *Writers INC* handbook, the importance of approaching writing as "mind traveling, destination unknown" is stressed. Determine what is meant by "mind traveling" by reading the introductory paragraphs in "The Writing Process" section. Then, in the space provided below, paraphrase (restate in your own words) this idea by completing the sentence starter.

Writing is ....

....

....

REVIEW: In addition to writing like a mind traveler, we also recommend that you . . .

(1) write about subjects that interest you,

(2) become knowledgeable about your subjects,

(3) share your work throughout the writing process,

(4) write with a purpose and audience in mind, and

(5) "speak" in an honest and sincere voice.

Note: We think all of these points are important when it comes to making writing a satisfying experience, an experience worth your time and effort, an experience that leads to something good.

WRITE: Now think carefully about your own process of completing writing assignments. Think of what you generally do first, second, third, and so on. Then, on your own paper, describe this process as clearly as you can. (It might help to focus your attention on the last few writing assignments you've completed.)

extend Compare your process of writing with the five points listed above. Do you normally write about subjects that interest you? Do you share your writing? Do you write with a purpose in mind and so on? (Share your thoughts with your classmates.)

Need a writing idea?

What's that? . . . You can't think of anything to write about? . . . Nothing ever happens to you? . . . Your life's about as exciting as low tide? (Not!) You have plenty to write about. Read on, and I'll prove it to you.

READ: Turn to the "Writing Topics" in our handbook and review the wide variety of writing ideas available to you just on this one page. (Refer to "Topics, Sample" in the handbook index for this information.)

REACT: In the space provided below, identify a possible writing idea for each general category listed under "Sample Writing Topics." (Share your results afterward.)

● Quotations:

● Descriptive: (Place)

● Narrative:

● Expository: (The causes of . . .)

● Persuasive:

WRITE: Write rapidly and freely for 5 minutes on your own paper focusing on one of the writing ideas you listed above. (Remember to write for the entire time. If you get stuck, write "I'm stuck" until something comes to mind.) When you've finished, you'll have proven to yourself that you do indeed have something to write about. (Share your results.)

extend List two other sections in the handbook that would be of help when you need a writing subject.

1.

2.

Free Writing for Ideas

READ: *"Free writing helps you think of topics to write about. Just keep writing, follow threads where they lead and you will get to ideas, experiences, feelings, and people that are just asking to be written about."* So says writer and teacher Peter Elbow. If you've tried free writing yourself, you know exactly what Mr. Elbow is talking about. Free writing is, in fact, the most immediate (and easiest) way to conduct a personal subject search. To review (or learn about) the steps involved in the free-writing process, read "Guidelines for Free Writing" in the handbook. (Refer to "Free writing" in the index for this information.)

REACT: Use the free-writing guidelines in your handbook to complete the following sentence starters: (Use these sentences as points of departure for a class discussion about free writing.)

1. Many things seem awkward or difficult when you first try them; free writing ....

....

2. Write nonstop and ....

....

3. Keep writing even when ....

....

4. Review your writing and underline ideas you like. These ideas will ....

....

WRITE: Let's suppose your teacher asked you to write an essay of information, that is, an essay in which you present facts and details about a current event, a community-related topic, a historical event, or any other factual subject you are interested in. Let's also suppose you're not sure what to write about, so you decide to try free writing to see if you can identify some possible writing ideas. (Grab a piece of paper and give it a try.)

Psst! How should you get started? Review the guidelines in the handbook. All you need to know is explained there. (Ask your teacher for possible writing prompts if you have trouble getting started. Afterward underline any potential writing ideas.)

Generating Texts

Could you be more specific?

READ: Let's suppose you're in the mood for a movie. You say to yourself, "Okay, what kind of movie will it be? Mystery? Adventure? Romance . . . ?" You decide on romantic adventure, something daring but realistic. You immediately rule out all of the Rambo-type movies. Instead, you focus your attention on the classic romantic film, say *Gone With the Wind*.

SELECT: Selecting a subject for writing should go much the same way. You start with a general area of interest (or your teacher provides one) and by carefully and thoughtfully chipping away at it, you form a specific subject to explore.

Psst! Why is this process important? It's difficult to develop a subject effectively if it is too broad. For example, you couldn't possibly write about movies in general (what would you say first or second or third?), but you could review Clark Gable's performance as Rhett Butler. That's specific enough to handle.

REACT: Put a check next to the subjects listed below that are too general to be covered in a typical writing assignment. (Share your results.)

- ○ Computers
- ○ Youth Employment
- ○ The Loss of My Best Friend, Mike
- ○ The Olympics
- ○ My Grandmother's Favorite Story

- ○ Women's Fashions
- ○ Nursing as a Career for Men
- ○ Playing the Not Dating Game
- ○ A Beautiful Night Turns Ugly
- ○ Hazardous Waste

WRITE: Carefully chip away at two of the general ideas you checked above until you come up with two specific subjects for writing. (Refer to "Selecting a subject" in the handbook index for help.) Share your selections with your classmates, as well as the process you used to make your selections.

1.

2.

inside info → Writing about a limited subject is important; writing about a subject that sincerely interests you is equally important. Keep both points in mind each time you begin a new writing project.

Where the Sidewalk Ends

We all know that writing is a journey, right? Well, some journeys follow sidewalks that are worn smooth by a thousand feet, and some journeys break new ground. Take a look at the following common writing topics:

- ● My Most Embarrassing Moment
- ● If I Wrote the Laws
- ● Me, Myself, and I—A Personal Interview
- ● The Biggest Change in My Life
- ● Why Go to School?

These sound like the old "sidewalk" topics, don't they? They might tempt you to write the same thing that everybody else writes. But wait! Your journey shouldn't stop there. It can take you beyond the place "where the sidewalk ends." How? Try brainstorming.

BRAINSTORM: Choose one of the five topics listed above (or make up one of your own).
Take between 5 and 10 minutes to brainstorm about it. Jot down a word or phrase for every single idea that comes into your mind. Don't reject any. **Suggestion:** Brainstorm out loud with a group of two to five classmates. Appoint one person to write down every idea that comes up.

Brainstorming Starters: If you have trouble starting or can't seem to keep going, ask yourself the following questions.

- ● Who? What? Where? When? Why? How? (These are the "5 W's and H.")
- ● What do I already know about this topic?
- ● What's the funny side? What's the serious side?
- ● What don't I know about the subject?
- ● Where can I find out more?
- ● Does this topic remind me of a story?

extend After your brain has stormed itself out, collect your best ideas and put them into
→ one sentence. Using that sentence as a starting point, begin free writing and keep it going for 5-8 minutes.

Personal Reflections

One thing that separates us human beings from the rest of the animal kingdom is our ability to wonder or reflect. We most often reflect upon or think about those things we hope for, wish for, or wonder about. We also reflect upon our feelings, our opinions, and what the future may bring. Because it occurs on such a personal level, reflective thinking provides an excellent source of ideas for writing and supplies us with an endless stream of details.

Examples:

> I hope to live to be a hundred.
>
> I wonder why they won't let students attend the meeting.
>
> I wish it would rain.
>
> I dream about traveling around the world.

REFLECT: Fill in the columns below with at least three *reflections* under each category. (Think and write freely. Don't worry about recording profound thoughts.)

I wish . . .	I hope . . .	I feel that . . .
I wonder . . .	I admire . . .	If only . . .

extend → Find a quiet spot where you can concentrate without interruption for at least 10 minutes. Reflect upon your life, your family, your friends, or your future during this time. Record your thoughts in your journal. Afterward, check those ideas that might be good to write about.

Ask the Write Questions

READ: Here is the opening paragraph of a student essay on a topic that almost everybody has something to say about, "My Room." Obviously, this writer knows her own bedroom better than any other person alive. But notice that she seems to have had trouble thinking of anything detailed, thoughtful, or important to say.

> My room is fairly clean. It's usually messy, but it just happens to be clean today. But under my bed is a real mess! So's the carpet because I never vacuum.

REFLECT: Think of your own bedroom. Would you have more to say about it than this? What makes your bedroom unlike any other? How much could you change your bedroom without losing the feeling that it is yours? How has your bedroom been changing lately?

WRITE: Go to your handbook and look up the list of "Structured Questions." (See "Writing process, Guidelines for shaping a subject" in the index.) Go through the questions one by one, making notes on whatever ideas they bring to mind. Then, choose two or three of these questions to answer in the space provided below.

Question/Answer: ....

....

Question/Answer: ....

....

Question/Answer: ....

....

Psst! When you've thought about all the structured questions listed in your handbook, make up some of your own to add to the list. For example, "Who else is interested in my room?" or "What feeling does my room give?" or "If my room were a boat, what would I name it, or where would I sail it?"

**inside
info** → Notice that right after the "Structured Questions," your handbook gives you a wackier set of "Offbeat (Unstructured) Questions." For a wilder spin to your writing, try those.

Creating a Plan of Action

READ: Read through the following two writing frameworks. Notice how the two sets of guidelines and directions compare to one another.

Writing Framework I: Write about an unforgettable incident or event that means something to you personally.
- **Subject:** An incident that means something to you personally (You decide.)
- **Purpose:** To share a personal story
- **Audience:** Your classmates
- **Form:** Paragraph or essay
- **Voice:** Informal and friendly

Writing Framework II: Write about an unforgettable incident or event that made you extremely angry or upset.
- **Subject:** Think of an incident that made you boil, turn 10 different shades of red, or see purple (Also make sure that your subject is appropriate for classroom use.)
- **Purpose:** To put the incident into perspective (or to get it out of your system)
- **Audience:** Yourself and your classmates
- **Form:** A letter addressed to another person involved in the incident
- **Voice:** Speak calmly and informally, or speak with emotion. (You decide.)

REACT: Both of these assignments focus on writing about an autobiographical incident, yet there obviously are major differences between the two. React to both assignments by answering the questions that follow: (Share responses.)

- Which assignment is more open-ended and general?

- Which assignment demands a bit more creativity and flair?

- Which assignment would you rather work on?

APPLY: Create another framework for writing about an autobiographical incident. Use the two samples above as your guide and include information about the *subject, purpose, audience, form,* and *voice.* For ideas, turn to "A Survey of Writing Forms" in the handbook. (Refer to "Forms, composition" in the index for this information.)

inside info → Your teacher may give you basic writing frameworks (like the two samples here) when she or he makes writing assignments. If not, consider creating your own. A framework will help you establish a basic focus and give you a set of guidelines to follow as you develop your writing.

Circling Around a Subject

READ: "Sooner or later you will feel the urge to say to your readers exactly what you think and what you alone are best suited to say about a particular subject. This idea or feeling should be your focus." So says the handbook in the opening statement under "Focusing Your Efforts." (Refer to "Focus" in the index for this information.) Read through the rest of this short but important discussion in the handbook; then complete the sentence starters below.

1. A focus is a ....

....

2. Write as many ....

....

3. A focus statement is often called ....

REVIEW: Your handbook provides a formula that works well for writing topic sentences that put a writing idea into focus. The formula is as follows:

> **Formula:** A specific subject (*Bungee jumping*) + a specific feeling or feature (*stretches safety to the limit*) = an effective focus statement for writing.

WRITE: Think of a specific subject for two of the general topics listed below. Then, on your own paper, form a focus statement for each subject, following the formula and model above.

● TV Shows:

● Fashions:

● Sports:

EXTEND: List three or four facts or details that support one of your focus statements. Use this information in a first draft of a paragraph or short essay. (Use your own paper for your work.)

inside info → Remember that a focus statement helps you decide upon a meaningful way to write about a subject. It creates a frame for your thinking, and it lets you know what is in bounds and out of bounds as you develop your work.

Designing a Writing Plan

Below you'll find a list of facts about political parties in the United States. Let's suppose these facts are the basic ingredients for a writing activity (perhaps an informative essay or paragraph). To get started, you need to decide what information to present to your audience and how to focus and deliver it.

REACT: Using "Designing a Writing Plan" in your handbook as a guide (refer to "Writing, Plan" in the index), answer the following questions about the list in preparation for your first draft: (Work on this activity with a partner if your teacher allows it.)

- What overall picture or pattern emerges as I read through the list? (And on a related note, what main feature or idea do I want to emphasize?)
- How will I develop my thoughts in my writing? (Will I provide a step-by-step history, an analysis, a comparison . . . ?)
- How will I organize my ideas? (What will I say first, second, and third? Will I need to prepare an outline or list to help organize my thoughts?)

Political Parties in the United States

1. The first two parties were the Federalist and the Democratic-Republican.
2. The Federalists were led by Alexander Hamilton.
3. The Democratic-Republicans were led by Thomas Jefferson.
4. The modern-day Democrats are descendants of the Democratic-Republicans.
5. The Democratic party is the oldest existing political party.
6. Between 1828 and 1860, Democrats won all but two presidential elections.
7. During the 1850's, the Democrats split over slavery.
8. Some Democrats supported slavery, others didn't.
9. In 1860, Abraham Lincoln became the first Republican president.
10. The Republican party started as an antislavery movement.
11. The Republican party won 14 of 18 presidential elections between 1860 and 1928.
12. The Republicans lost popularity after the big stock-market crash of 1929.
13. Because of financial scandals and insecurity, the Republicans won little support between 1933 and 1952.
14. Democrat Franklin D. Roosevelt was elected president four times during that period.
15. Dwight D. Eisenhower was elected in 1952.
16. He was the first Republican president in 24 years.
17. The Democrats won the presidency in 1960, 1964, and 1976.
18. Republicans held it between 1980 and 1992.
19. The Democrats controlled both houses of Congress from 1986 to 1994.

---

extend Write an exploratory (rough) draft about our political parties, focusing your attention on whatever idea or feature you want to stress.

Getting Your Facts Straight

Once you decide on a specific course of action for your writing, you must consider what you are going to say first, second, third, and so on. Sometimes the order in which things should be presented is obvious and demands no special planning. However, with longer essays for which you've gathered a great deal of information, planning an orderly arrangement of ideas becomes important. That's where outlining (or another organizing strategy like *listing*, *clustering*, or *mapping*) comes into play.

REVIEW: Review the section on outlining in the handbook. (Refer to "Outlining, Compositions" in the index to find this information.) Carefully note how the subject of "Paper Recycling" is broken down into manageable units in the sample outline.

APPLY: Let's assume you've gathered the list of facts below for a paragraph about surface mining. Organize the information related to this type of mining into an outline. (**Hint:** The first fact listed will be your only Roman numeral.) Do your work on your own paper and make sure to share your results.

Mining

- Surface-mining methods are practiced when mineral or ore deposits are located at or near the earth's surface.
- Placer mining is one method of surface mining.
- Placer mining is used to get gold and other heavy minerals from gravel.
- Dredging is used where layers of gravel are especially thick.
- In placer mining, gold and other heavy minerals are sifted out using water.
- A dredging machine brings up buckets of water-softened gravel.
- Strip mining is a third surface method.
- Dredging is another surface method.
- In dredging, the heavy minerals are sifted out of the gravel and sand.
- Strip mining is used to obtain coal, phosphate, and other minerals.
- In strip mining, furrows are cut in the earth's surface to get at the minerals and ores.

---

inside info → When you outline, the purpose is not to produce neatly packaged units of thought. Outlining is simply one strategy that can help you organize your thoughts as you develop your writing. Make it work for you.

The First Go 'Round

All right, you've gathered some facts, you've got some ideas about the purpose and audience for your writing. You've done a little planning and organizing. And you've got a blank piece of paper in front of you. You're ready to write a first draft. What's the best way to proceed from here?

READ: Read the "Writing the First Draft" section in your handbook (it's in the opening chapter) and find out for yourself how to begin. Make note of at least two things you've learned about writing first drafts. (Share your results below.)

1. ....

   ....

2. ....

   ....

REACT & WRITE: Look carefully at the writing framework that follows. Then gear yourself up. You're going to write a first draft for a pet peeve, keeping in mind what you just learned about writing first drafts. Afterward, share your results. Consider how closely you and your partner followed the handbook guidelines.

Assignment: Write a pet peeve, a short paper in which you discuss something in your everyday life that bugs you. (*Noisy eaters, mindless busywork,* etc.)

- **Subject:** (Your choice)

- **Purpose:** To inform and/or entertain

- **Audience:** Your classmates

- **Form:** A brief personal essay (paragraph)

- **Voice:** Informal or familiar

inside info → Remember that a first draft is your first look at a writing idea. Your goal should be to produce *possibilities* rather than perfection, so write freely and openly.

Developing Texts

Writing *About* Rather Than Around

"About" is a funny little word . . . a preposition, actually. It used to mean "around," such as "I was walking about the mall." Nowadays, it isn't often used to mean that; but sometimes it seems like "about" still means "around" when it comes to writing about a person. That is, it's difficult to capture the full or real person in writing. Very often, writers only manage to write *around* a person, rather than capture what that person is really all about.

READ: How can you avoid such a trap? Your handbook knows . . . Read the guidelines provided there for describing a person. (Refer to "Writing, About a person" in the index.) Apply what you have learned in this section by describing a classmate or relative (with his or her approval, of course). Note below at least one detail for each suggestion (or as many as possible) listed in the handbook guidelines.

1. Observe:

2. Investigate:

3. Define:

4. Describe:

5. Recall:

6. Compare:

7. Analyze:

8. Evaluate:

WRITE: Write a first draft of a description of a person—working in details from above as you go along. Share your first draft with a partner. Then continue working with your description until you feel it captures your subject.

inside info → Your handbook provides guidelines for writing about a PERSON, a PLACE, an OBJECT, and an EVENT. Make use of these guidelines whenever you need help gathering details for your writing. (Also note the guidelines for writing explanations and writing to persuade.)

In Support

There's a certain level or depth of detail that readers expect in a piece of writing. When a point is made, they expect it to be fully explained with specific examples and details before the next important point is made. The act of presenting readers with important points and then supporting these points with details and examples is the core of almost all types of writing.

READ: Read the paragraph below. It is a skeleton of a basic expository paragraph containing a topic sentence followed by four important points. What the paragraph does not contain is supporting ideas, details, and examples.

SUPPORT: Put some flesh on the bones of this paragraph by adding supporting ideas and details after each major point. Space has been provided below for your planning. Then write an expanded paragraph (or short essay) on your own paper. *Note:* Two supporting ideas after each point are almost always better than one.

> Saturday morning cartoons helped to shape the way I think. 1. Most of them taught me never to take life too seriously. 2. In an offhanded sort of way, they have provided me with a guide on how to act. 3. They've also influenced the type of movies and books I like to read. 4. I'd even go so far as to say that they have influenced the way I look at Saturday mornings as a young adult.

1. ....

   ....

2. ....

   ....

3. ....

   ....

4. ....

   ....

extend Share the results of your writing. Review each other's writing to make sure the details support the main idea. For instance, did you include a specific cartoon example? If not, your piece is probably still too general.

2, 3, 1 Contact!

There are several ways to arrange details in your writing so that you get and hold your reader's attention. Here are three basic patterns:

1. The 1-2-3 pattern of arrangement presents information from most to least important and is a pattern with which most of you are familiar.

2. The 3-2-1 pattern arranges information from least to most important. Use it if you want to build steadily to a climax.

3. The 2-3-1 pattern is the most rhythmic and flexible: it starts with something quite surprising (or important), moves to something a little less surprising, and ends with something most surprising of all.

Each pattern results in a different effect, and it's up to you to select the one that best serves your purpose.

REARRANGE: Below is a paragraph organized in a 1-2-3 arrangement of details. Rearrange the paragraph into the 2-3-1 pattern, and put this new version on your own paper. (Rearrange the supporting details in the paragraph. Leave the two opening sentences and the closing sentence alone. Make any other changes necessary for smooth reading.)

Most people think of smokestacks and car fumes when they think of air pollution. However, we are exposed to more air pollution when we are inside our own homes than when we are outside inhaling more noticeable factory fumes. The biggest reason why in-home air is so polluted is the lack of air circulation. As we try to make our houses airtight in order to keep our heating and cooling costs down, we trap air inside the house. We then continue to recirculate that air behind airtight windows and doors until it becomes stale and dust filled. Another reason is that we use home products without realizing that they're air polluters. Products such as personal deodorants, hair spray, cooking gas, and cleaning fluids pollute our air. And people themselves pollute the air. We all emit "bioeffluents," chemicals such as butyric acid, ethyl alcohol, and carbon dioxide. So the next time you feel an irresistible urge to fight air pollution, open a window.

 **extend** Write a paragraph or an essay on any topic using the 2-3-1 method of arrangement. → Share your results!

Tucking in Definitions

READ: Below is a passage from a high-school student's essay titled "The Surf Culture." Notice how he defines any surfer slang words that the reader probably won't know.

What do you do when you know a word that your reader probably doesn't? Do you use it and risk losing the reader? Do you skip the word and substitute a more familiar synonym? Or do you use the word along with a helpful definition, tucked in so that the sentence flows smoothly through it? If you are writing to inform your reader, the third way is usually the best.

. . . A surfer begins his surfing life at a young age as a "grommet." Surfers beginning at an older age are known as "kooks" or "barneys." A grommet is generally an overly enthusiastic annoyance who sticks surf stickers all over the back of Mom's car and drools at meager, tiny surf. It is an uphill battle for the kook or grommet because of continuous abuse from the respected surfers. As a surfer becomes old (over 40), he may become a "guru." This character is an old, weathered expert who has 20 boards in the rafters of his garage and can tell you for hours about how much better it was before you were born.

REFLECT: Check over the "surfer" paragraph carefully, noticing how each sentence works. Then take this little true or false quiz.

True or *False*

.... **1.** The writer handles all definitions in a similar fashion.

.... **2.** All the sentences first offer the new word and then give a definition.

.... **3.** The new word is surrounded by quotation marks every time it is used.

.... **4.** Every definition appears in the same sentence as the word it defines.

REACT: Compare your answers with someone else's. Think about your observations, and write a brief summary of what they've taught you about tucking in definitions.

WRITE: Think of some specialized vocabulary that you know. Maybe it's skateboard slang, the language of needlepoint, or the special terminology used in CB radio. Write a paragraph to inform a newcomer about your subject. In your paragraph, use at least three new terms and smoothly tuck in their definitions.

inside info →

If you are writing to readers who probably know much more about your subject than you do, you usually don't need to give definitions. For superior readers, define only those words that you want to give an unusual or personal twist. For readers such as little children, who are quite far below your level of intelligence or experience, either be very obvious with your definitions or substitute simpler words.

Psst! For more on writing definitions, look up "Definition, Guidelines for writing" in the index of your handbook.

Using Sensory Details

READ: Below is a paragraph about a grandmother's house by a Jamaican writer, Michelle Cliff. Read to enjoy, but also notice the rich variety of details.

Note: Details are the specific ideas you use to flesh out the main points in a piece of writing. If you look in the handbook index under "Details, Kinds of," you will find a section that describes three different kinds of detail. Make yourself thoroughly familiar with all three: ● Sensory ● Memory ● Reflective

> Her house had four rooms, no electricity, no running water. The kitchen was a shed in the back with a small pot-bellied stove. Across from the stove was a mahogany counter, which had a white enamel basin set into it. The only light source was a window, a small space covered partly by a wooden shutter. We washed our faces and hands in enamel bowls with cold water carried in kerosene tins from the river and poured from enamel pitchers. Our chamber pots were enamel also, and in the morning we carefully placed them on the steps at the side of the house where my grandmother collected them and disposed of their contents. The outhouse was about thirty yards from the back door—a "closet" as we called it, infested with lizards capable of changing color. When the door was shut it was totally dark, and the lizards made their presence known by the noise of their scurrying through the torn newspaper, or the soft shudder when they dropped from the walls. I remember most clearly the stench of the toilet, which seemed to hang in the air in that climate.

REFLECT: Notice how smoothly some details fit into their sentences. Record some of the details that bring this passage alive for you.

....

....

....

WRITE: To practice some detailed writing of your own, first stare at something a very short distance away. (A book, folder, poster, hairdo, etc.) Look at it for quite some time until you are thoroughly absorbed in it and have forgotten about everything else. Write a paragraph full of fine detail, telling what, in your imagination, you see.

Using Repetition

Some repetition of words or ideas is boring and unnecessary, as when I write, "His bald head was totally without hair." We call that redundancy. But some repetition can be useful. For instance, when I want to keep the focus of my paragraph fixed on one thing or create a feeling of intensity in the writing, I can repeat an important feature.

READ: Here is a portion of writing by a student who has used repetition effectively:

My writing has become a way for me to think and discover who I am. I am a sensitive person who cares about the quality of life for others and the environment. I am someone who loves the coast of Maine and who works to preserve it. I am an optimist because I try to look at all possibilities, but I am a pessimist, too, because my perceptions of the world around me often don't meet my expectations.

REACT: Here are some questions to help you digest what you've just read:

● Which words are repeated?

● Does the repetition of "I am" sound too self-centered?

● Would repetition like this work better in a speech than in writing, or vice versa?

● How many sentences beginning with "I am" do you think you could write without losing energy?

WRITE: Compose a paragraph or two in which you repeat the words "I am" at or near the beginning of most of the sentences. Finish the thoughts any way you want. If you wish, create a repeated pattern using different words.

inside info →

When careful writers repeat words, they are usually trying to create a special effect. They make the series get louder and louder, softer and softer, closer and closer, or maybe more and more angry. Sometimes the series of repetitions will build up and then taper off. See what you can do.

Typecasting Paragraphs

There are as many different kinds of paragraphs as there are writers, because the style, organization, and general feel of a paragraph reflect a writer's unique way of forming and expressing his or her thoughts. However, there are four basic types of paragraphs that young writers are often asked to work with in their school-related writing. Your handbook provides a discussion and model for each type.

READ: Review the "Types of Paragraphs" section in the handbook. (Refer to "Paragraph, Types of" in the index.) Pay special attention to the models.

REACT: Answer the following questions based on your reading of the model paragraphs. (Share your answers.)

1. Does the model *descriptive* paragraph describe a person's actions, appearance, or personality?

2. What type of paragraph would you write if you were to share a personal experience?

3. What does *narrate* mean?

4. An *expository* paragraph presents ....

5. What other section(s) of the handbook is recommended for more information about expository writing?

6. What are the two primary parts of a *persuasive* paragraph?
   a.
   b.

7. What type of paragraph is easiest for you to write?

8. What type of paragraph is most difficult for you to write?

REVIEW: Reread what the handbook has to say about one of the types of paragraphs. Then find at least two other pieces of information in the handbook that would help you write this type of paragraph. (Read this information carefully and share your findings.)

It Goes Without Saying

If you've been told that every paragraph should have a topic sentence to unify the paragraph, that's generally true. However, some paragraphs successfully communicate an overall idea without actually stating it, especially in stories or narratives. An opening topic sentence sometimes might undermine the paragraph's emotional appeal. Or it might take away some of the readers' pleasure in discovering the main idea for themselves.

READ: Here is a paragraph lifted from an essay by a talented student writer. As you enjoy this description of bicycling in the French Pyrenees, notice that the paragraph has no topic sentence:

> The road steepened considerably, however, and Tom and Keith pedaled away from me. Brian was somewhat closer to me, and eventually I caught up to him and the two of us continued to climb out of the gorge, riding up the side of a valley sheathed in short, green grass. The road buckled up and down, never maintaining a constant pitch, preventing me from getting into a good climbing rhythm. This was little consolation, however, when David, whom we had left behind miles ago on the flats, came whistling by the two of us just past the tiny town of St. Engrace. Brian and I cursed through our teeth, and inched our way up to a somewhat flat section halfway up the climb.

REACT: Even though you can't find a topic sentence in this paragraph, you will find a main idea and a feeling or attitude about it that you will carry through the paragraph and on to the next one. Record your discoveries below.

- Main idea: ....

....

....

- Feeling or attitude: ....

....

....

WRITE: On your own paper, write a paragraph about a journey you've taken. Don't begin at the beginning, but place yourself somewhere in the middle of the action or experience so that you communicate a central idea and related feeling or attitude without capturing it in a single topic sentence.

Reviewing Texts

Teamwork Works!

Basketball and writing group workshops have at least five things in common. First, both are team efforts: members depend on each other, and if anybody slacks off, the whole team suffers. Second, participants have to be prepared: a forward who's late getting down the floor can blow a fast break, and a writer who hasn't done his or her homework blows the chance for everybody to learn from that work. Third, it's frustrating playing with a guard who's a ball hog for the same reason that it's boring working with a writer who participates only when his or her essay is discussed. Fourth, teammates in both groups benefit when they care enough about themselves—and each other—to give and to take constructive criticism. And finally, doing a good job in either activity costs something, but the payback is worth it!

REVIEW: Review the section "Writing Group Guidelines" in your handbook. (Refer to "Group skills, Writing" in the index to find this information.)

RECORD: Record two or three things that you really need to keep in mind both as a writer and as a responder. This will be your short checklist of reminders when you work in a writing group. (Share your results.)

As a Writer

1. ....

2. ....

3. ....

As a Responder

1. ....

2. ....

3. ....

APPLY: Using this checklist, review a recent piece of writing in a group of three to five classmates. Make sure that everyone contributes to the cause.

inside info → Sometimes working in pairs is a great icebreaker for writers not experienced with writing groups. The same rules and guidelines apply, only on a much more limited scale.

Small (Group) Talk

Most writers like to get direct feedback from their peers, the kind one gets in a small writing group. But a fairly large number will tell you that they don't care at all for the comments their fellow students write.

READ: What kind of comments are the most helpful? Here are some lifted directly from the paper of a student who wrote an essay about a bicycle trip he had taken with some friends along the route of the Tour de France. In their comments, his classmates show quite different attitudes and aims, as you will see:

(1) Wow Dave, I didn't know you had it in you! I certainly could not have done that! What a feeling of accomplishment. Great setup and story. Seriously consider this for publication.

Georgia

(2) Quite an interesting story, at least to me. Personally, I think it needs a paragraph discussing the various equipment you and your fellow riders used, but that would probably bore your audience. A really neat setting for a story. I think you might want to focus more on the trip as an "exciting race" rather than a journey. More description of the mountain scenery would also be neat. The climbing part was very well written.

Don B.

(3) Great! Your story made me feel the way I did when I won a race in swimming once. Super tired at the end, but happy. I love that feeling, but you can only get it if you suffer for it somehow. You've got to give something up. Thanks for reminding me.

Rico

(4) I'm not into biking so I don't have much to say about this. The beginning didn't do much for me. Oh well. I like more science fiction stuff. Why'd you put the jokes in near the end? They're lame. But don't take it personal. I'm just grouchy today.

Dena

REFLECT: What different approaches do you see in these four comments? Think about questions such as these: Is each set of comments encouraging or discouraging? Is each one personal or impersonal? Is it emotional or thoughtful? Is it helpful or unhelpful? Is it general or specific? After you've thought about the student comments using the questions above, rank them from most helpful and encouraging to least helpful. Briefly explain what is good or not so good about each comment. (Share your results.)

Ranked First: ⬭ Why? ....

....

....

Ranked Second: ⬭ Why? ....

....

....

Ranked Third: ⬭ Why? ....

....

....

Ranked Fourth: ⬭ Why? ....

....

....

Psst! If you have trouble commenting on these responses, review "Group Advising and Revising" in the handbook. (Refer to "Group skills, Writing" in the index for this information.)

inside info → Remember: Give praise when praise is due when you are commenting on your classmates' work, but base your praise on something you specifically observe or feel in the writing. Writing sessions should not be popularity contests.

Good Writing: A Matter of Choice

What makes for good writing? Six basic points appear on the lists of most writing experts: Good writing is . . .

- **original** (the subject or the way the subject is covered is lively and energized),
- **organized** (the ideas are presented in a sensible order),
- **detailed** (the details are specific and colorful),
- **clear** (the sentences clearly and smoothly move the writing forward),
- **correct** (the final product is clean and correct), and
- **effective** (the writing is interesting and informative).

What makes writing work for you? Let's find out.

READ: Carefully read the sample paragraphs that follow. (All three are excerpts from student essays.) Consider underlining words or ideas that you especially like and drawing a wavy line under words or ideas that confuse you. Then rank the paragraphs (1, 2, 3) putting a "1" next to the paragraph you like best.

Note: Base your ranking on the markings you have made, the qualities of good writing described above, and your own gut feeling about the passages. Even a piece of writing that has problems can be good writing at the heart of things—a diamond in the rough.

We were outside, walking around looking for something to do. I saw an old bomb shelter.

I dared Junior to go in. He said that he would go in if I would. We walked up closer to it. Finally, we were at the entrance. When I opened the door, it creaked. Inside we saw a dusty, dreary room at the far end of a tunnel, so we decided to see what was in it. I faintly heard water dripping as we walked down the tunnel. We found a few candles and some old crates in the room. As we turned to leave, Junior tripped on a beam, and the small room started to give. We ran like the dickens. By the time we got to the other end of the tunnel, the small room had completely collapsed. We were lucky to be alive.

During recess we played with the boys all of the time. We were just as good as they were in all of the "team sports," and they knew it. In spring and fall we played kickball, keep away, and smear; but it was in the winter that the best and the worst came out in us. Almost every day we held a massive snowball fight. What generally started out as a flurry of innocent snowballs lofted in high arcs would, in a matter of minutes, transform into an uninhibited free-for-all. Some snowballs whizzed past unprotected heads; others hit their mark. Face washings came from every direction. Hats, zipped jackets, and boots were signs of weakness. This was a game for the young and the reckless. The only compromise to comfort was in our hand wear. Snowmobile mittens reigned supreme! They kept our hands dry, and they packed a nasty snowball. After recess the combing of wet heads splattered desk tops while snow on our jeans melted into puddles on the floor. All afternoon the hallways smelled like a wool-dyeing factory. Teachers did everything they could think of to get us to stop, but we never listened. We were having too much fun.

My brother and I got into the roller coaster and locked ourselves in. We started to move and slowly submerged into the Demon's first tunnel. I felt like I was the camera on one of those National Geographic specials, going into the mouth of some strange creature. Then we went straight up and straight down. It was . . . AAAAAHHHHH! Coming around the corner and down, down, down the hill! Over the loop-de-loops (twice even)! Screaming and yelling all the way! Around the corner again, leaning! Muscles tightening, stomach growling! My facelifting, squashing! My brain going bonkers! All the bones in my body were . . . We started to slow down and then stopped. As I walked down the exit ramp, I heard a guy say, "Enjoy your ride?"

I turned and looked at him and said to myself, "Yeah, right."

extend Share the results of your ranking with your classmates. Then discuss the reasons for one of your selections in a paragraph. In your discussion, refer to specific things you liked or disliked in the writing. The object here is not to come to a consensus about what good writing is, but to share your sensibilities about writing.

Pretty Well Written

READ: Read and enjoy the paragraph that follows. Make note of parts of the paragraph you especially like as well as parts that you have questions about.

Mrs. Ritzy's Pride

When I was little, my mother taught me how important it is for everyone to throw garbage into trash cans. No matter where we were, or how we were dressed, if my mother saw a piece of paper, a soda can, or any bit of garbage on the sidewalk, she would pick it up and carry it to the next available trash can. One time we were in Manhattan during spring break, and Mother and I were wearing our Easter finery—white gloves, hats, new shoes, new coats, the works—when she spotted a richly dressed woman throw a half-eaten pretzel on the sidewalk. Naturally, Mother picked up the remains and started towards the nearest garbage can—or so I thought. The next thing I knew, she was standing toe-to-toe with Mrs. Ritzy. "Excuse me, but I believe you lost something," said my mother, handing the pretzel to the woman. The woman looked down her long, expensive nose. "Whut deed you say?" My mother shook her finger disapprovingly, pulled herself up to her full five feet, and in a voice dripping with sarcasm replied, "I said, 'I believe you lost something,' and I was right. When you throw your garbage on the sidewalk for everyone to see, you throw away your pride. Now take your 'pride' and see to it that it's put in the right place." I was sure that Mrs. Ritzy was going to bop Mother over the head with her designer handbag. Instead, she meekly took the half-chewed pretzel and escorted it to a nearby trash can. To this day, whenever I see someone littering, I think, pretty is as pretty does.

REACT: Answer the following questions about the sample paragraph. Make sure to review the paragraph before you respond to each question. (Refer to "Paragraph" in the handbook index for more information about this form.

yes | no

Topic Sentence:
Does the paragraph contain a clearly stated (or implied) topic sentence? (An effective topic sentence generally identifies the subject of the writing as well as a specific feeling or impression about that subject.)

yes | no

Content:

Is the paragraph unified? (That is, do all of the sentences that follow support the topic sentence?)

Do the supporting sentences say enough about the topic sentence? (Are there enough supporting details, examples, or steps in these sentences to answer all of a reader's questions?)

Form:

Are the sentences organized or arranged in the best possible order? (And do the sentences move logically and smoothly from one point to the next?)

Does the paragraph come to an effective conclusion? (That is, does the paragraph come to a natural stopping point, or does a concluding sentence effectively tie any loose ends together?)

Style:

Does the writer's voice match his or her purpose? (That is, do the writer's words and manner of "speaking" match the subject of his or her writing? Serious subjects should be treated seriously and lighter subjects more informally and casually.)

Has the writer given proper attention to word choice, interesting details, and sentence style? (That is, does the writer use nouns that are specific, verbs that are vivid, and descriptive words and phrases that are colorful and helpful? And do the sentences read well?)

WRITE: State the overall strengths and weaknesses of the sample paragraph, using your responses to the questions above as your guide. (Share your results.)

Overall Strengths and Weaknesses: ....

....

....

....

....

....

....

....

Essay in Review

READ: Read the student essay below. Take note of the passages you like and don't like. Then answer the questions that follow on the next page.

1
2
3
4
    I've always wished that I could be one of those people who never has to study yet still manages to get good grades. Since I'm not, I not only have to study, but study hard. Over the years, though, I've developed some habits which I have found very useful in studying for tests.

5
6
7
8
9
10
11
    First, it's important to find out what a teacher emphasizes on a test. Unless you can talk to someone who took the course before you, this may have to wait until after the first test, but it makes studying much easier if you know that most of the test material is taken from either the textbook, the teacher's notes, or some other source. I once had a teacher who was very unpredictable when it came to tests. Along with this, take notice of what kind of test is usually given. Different techniques of study can be used for objective tests such as multiple choice or true/false as compared to essay exams.

12
13
14
15
16
    Second, always start studying early and never cram for a test. Even after cramming for a test, a teacher can catch you with some little-mentioned fact. What works best for me is to read the material well before the test, take notes, and review the notes every day until the test. In this way I'm not up all night studying before a test, but getting a good night's sleep.

17
18
19
20
21
    Third, make use of memory crutches. Flash cards are not just for first-graders. They are a simple yet effective way to help recall facts. Or to help remember ideas. Also, you can run through flash cards at any time, whenever you have a couple of spare minutes. I also find that writing hard-to-remember facts down on paper reinforces them in my mind. Also, any kind of word association that helps in remembering can be used.

22
23
24
    These ideas, which have become regular habits for me, could work for you. I can't guarantee getting good grades if followed, but just the added effort put forth toward your studies will most likely show definite improvements.

REACT: After reading the essay, answer the following questions. (Refer to "A Checklist for Critiquing a Paper" in your handbook for help. Look under "Writing process, Group advising and revising" in the index.)

1. What is good or interesting about this student essay?

2. What are some of its overall weaknesses?

3. List six problems (or as many as you can) in the essay that relate to originality, the arrangement and smooth flow of ideas, the effective use of details, word choice, clarity, variety, and so on. Identify the area of the problem by using the line numbers located in the left margin of the essay.

a. ....

....

b. ....

....

c. ....

....

d. ....

....

e. ....

....

f. ....

....

extend Share your reviews with at least two classmates. How are your observations similar? How are they different?

Revising Texts

Draft Report

Your writing will never satisfy you or reflect the best that you can do if you don't put a great deal of effort into rewriting and revising. The following often quoted comment speaks well to this point: "There is no such thing as good writing, only good rewriting."

READ: Consider the following draft of an assignment in which students were asked to describe a memorable person, focusing on his or her appearance and/or actions.

Ted

When I was a kid, there was this guy who worked for my father who used to hang around. My father built houses and fixed up people's kitchens and stuff. Ted worked for my father off and on for about five years. He would work until he got enough money to live for a while without working. Then he'd come back around to make some more money. Beats me what he did when he wasn't working for us. He painted and straightened nails and hauled equipment, and other stuff. He was 61 and he lived in a Crown Victoria car with maroon leather upholstery. He had a funny patchwork quilt and lace pillows in the backseat. It looked just like a living room for little people. He even had a little TV that hooked up to his car's lighter. He parked the car on his brother's farm. On sunny days, he'd open up the trunk where he kept a cooler, take out a lawn chair, and sit there sipping root beer. I don't know what else he did. It was funny to see him pull up in his house every morning, his blue eyes sparkling, his Chicago Cubs baseball hat pushed back on his balding head. After a cup of coffee, he'd say to my father, "Well I guess I need a few more chores, Tony."

REACT: Let's suppose that this is your first draft. How would you go about revising this writing? You could begin by reading the introduction to "Revising" in the first chapter of the handbook for ideas. (Refer to "Revising" in the index if you have trouble finding this information.)

APPLY: Four questions contained in the introduction are listed here. Provide answers for each one as they relate to the sample description. (Use your own paper and share your results.)

- Is the content interesting and worth sharing?
- Is the style natural and effective in getting my message across?
- Are there any major gaps or soft spots in my writing?
- How can I improve what I have done so far?

extend Apply the questions above to one of your own first drafts. Make changes accordingly as you revise.

Cut, Clarify, Condense

Would you like an easy and effective strategy for fixing problems with wording? All you have to do is use the "Editing Code" below to help you *cut, clarify,* and *condense.*

- CUT [brackets]
  If you find a part that's unnecessary or off the subject, put brackets around it. If you decide that section is really unneeded, cut it!
- CLARIFY 〰️
  If you find something confusing, unclear, or incomplete in your writing, put a wavy line under that section. You should rethink, reword, explain, or add detail.
- CONDENSE (parentheses)
  If you come across a section of your writing that is wordy or overexplained, put a set of parentheses around it.

READ: Here's a portion of a student essay still in progress. (For the sake of this activity, suppose this is your writing.) Read the draft carefully and evaluate it using the 3-C's revising code. (Also try to make some constructive comments as you go along.)

Stand By Your Fort

I've met a lot of people in school, and some of them were memorable. Some were good friends, some were enemies, and some made brief appearances but left no impressions. Sometimes on cold, snowy days when I catch a glimpse of a half-built snow fort, I think to myself, "Whatever happened to Kendall Klip, the most feared girl in third grade?" Kendall wasn't too popular with us, but her words carried weight because she was Kendall, the awesome girl-bully. She was as tough as her nickname, and she had done a lot to earn it. I remember the one time we spent all of our recess time for a week building a snow fort. That project consumed all of our playtime. That was also the week of the winter carnival. I remember Mary Osmond and I were on the decoration committee. We must have made hundreds of paper carnations. When our fort was all done, Kendall came along and said it was hers. We told her to go fly a kite, but she was determined to take command of our fort. She also said that if we didn't give it up peacefully, she would knock it down. Everyone decided in the best interest of the fort to temporarily leave it. Everyone except me that is. Instead, I just went up to that rude girl, looked into her eyes (which were about six inches above mine), and told her exactly what I thought of her.

extend Discuss the results of your review with at least one classmate. (It's always interesting to discover how someone else sees the same piece of writing.) Then talk about the specific changes you would make in this piece of writing.

Energize Your Writing

A well-written paragraph is like a refurbished 1969 Mustang fastback—it appeals to the senses, all the senses. It's smooth and inviting, agile and colorful. Its machinery purrs along gracefully. You can even smell the leather upholstery and feel the steering wheel in your hands.

This may seem like an odd comparison, but writing—like a 1969 Mustang fastback—should appeal to the senses and be inviting, tempting, even thrilling. Using concrete nouns, vivid verbs, and colorful adjectives can help give your writing these qualities.

SHOW: The paragraph below is technically correct—but drab. Energize it by substituting specific, descriptive words for the underlined ho-hum words. Also feel free to rearrange and add sentences as you rewrite the paragraph. (Use the space provided below for your work.)

Psst! It might help to think in terms of SHOWING rather than TELLING. Show us what it is you're talking about; don't just tell us.

My uncle Telio's car is great. It looks cool, and it's fun to ride in. That's because Uncle Telio is a unique driver. Some people go to amusement parks for an enjoyable ride. I just hang out with my uncle.

....

....

....

....

....

....

....

....

extend Team up with a partner and read your paragraphs out loud. Take note of the showing details and overall effectiveness of each other's work.

Working with Transitions

Eating one candy bar is satisfying; eating too many is sickening. One sentence with a transitional word at the beginning may seem like good writing style, but a whole series of sentences, all beginning with short introductory transitional words—well, you get the idea. (For a list of the commonly used transitions, refer to "Transitions, Useful linking expressions" in the handbook index.)

READ: Keep your eye on the sentence openings as you read this carefully written student response to a well-known short story.

Gifts of Love

In O'Henry's story, "The Gift of the Magi," the author proves through the actions of Della and Jim that those who act with selfless love are the wisest. For example, those who truly love can give away those things they hold dearest to ensure the other's happiness. Specifically, Della sells her long, silky hair to buy a new gold chain for Jim's pocket watch. Simultaneously, Jim sells the pocket watch his father had given him to buy Della the tortoiseshell combs she has been admiring. In summary, each sacrifices his or her most precious possession so that the other will be happy. Sadly, the couple discover the ironic event. They seem heartbroken. However, Della and Jim soon realize that their actions were prompted because of the love they have for each other. As can be seen, love is worth great sacrifice.

REACT: Would you agree that too many sentences in this paragraph begin in the same way, with a single introductory word? Do you feel yourself wanting to scream, or at least put some of your editing skills to work?

REWORK: Here is a way to rework the sentence openings so they draw less attention to themselves.

- CIRCLE all the transitional words and phrases.
- CROSS OUT any that aren't needed.
- TUCK some of them into the sentence if you can find a natural "breathing space" for them. In other words, find a place near the beginning of the sentence where the word fits in smoothly.
- CHANGE some of the remaining words into phrases or clauses.
- LEAVE the rest just as they are.

WRITE: After you have thought through all of the transition changes you would make, rewrite the paragraph so it reads more smoothly and effectively. (Watch for unnecessary repetition.)

....

....

....

....

....

....

....

....

....

....

....

....

....

....

....

....

....

....

extend Listening to good writing is like listening to good music: in both experiences, we're often drawn into the content (words) by the rhythm. A varied, interesting rhythm grabs and holds our attention—while it gives us pleasure. Look back at the openings of your sentences above. Is there variety in the rhythm? Did you make music for the reader?

If Endings Could Talk

The ending of an essay can say much more than "Th-th-th-that's all, folks!"

The truth is, though, that many of us get stuck on the idea that endings are easy: all we have to do (we think) is repeat our main point. That's seldom the case. Successful endings can say many things besides "That's all, folks" or "Here's my main point for (yawn) the last time" or "In summary, . . ."

Here's the last paragraph of a student's essay about the famous, eccentric billionaire Howard Hughes. What does it seem to be saying?

> . . . Though he died over fifteen years ago, the legend of Howard Hughes lives on. He represented the American Dream turned on itself, a victim of the multibillion-dollar empire which he almost single-handedly created. We will always be fascinated by celebrities, heroes, the wealthy, and the sick. Howard was all of these. And more.

READ: This ending sums up the story of Howard Hughes by saying, in effect, "Weird, isn't it?" It tells us that our interest in certain celebrities is natural—they'll always get under our skin. Other endings say similar things. If you would take a quick tour through a collection of fine essays, listening to the endings "talk," here are some of the things you would hear the last paragraphs say: (Read through this list carefully.)

- Oh, well . . .
- It all comes down to this: . . .
- Best of all, . . . (or Worst of all, . . .)
- And one more thing . . .
- Here we go 'round again . . .
- In fact, the opposite is true . . .
- As I think about it now, . . .
- As so-and-so has said, . . .
- And why not?
- If that's what you want, then here's what you do . . .
- And this has been my point all along . . .
- I'll say it here for the last time . . .
- And would you believe it, . . .
- But it comes out okay . . .
- It's a strange world, isn't it?
- And here's the difference . . .
- The secret is to . . .
- That's the problem . . .
- And now it's your turn . . .
- But despite everything, . . .

REFLECT: Think of a time in your life when something came to an end, like your love of drawing, your fear of failure, your piano lessons, or whatever. Imagine you have just written an essay about that time. Then in the space below, write two different endings to that essay. Let each ending say one of the things on the list, such as "In fact, the opposite is true" or "As so-and-so has said, . . ." (You could also write two different endings to a piece of writing you have already completed if that would be easier for you.)

extend For an extra challenge, how about choosing one of the statements in the list on the previous page and using it as your guide for rewriting the "Howard Hughes" conclusion?

Refining:
Sentence Strengthening

Double Whammy

Most sentences contain several basic ideas that work together to form a complete thought. For example, if you were to write a sentence about a power failure that struck your school (don't you wish!) causing a number of problems, you might be working with at least six different ideas. Each of these ideas could be written as a separate sentence.

1. There was a power failure.
2. The power failure hit the school.
3. The power failure hit without warning.
4. The failure left the lower-level classes completely in the dark.
5. The failure left the tech-ed classes without operable equipment.
6. The failure left the cafeteria staff with a pile of half-cooked hot dogs.

REVIEW: An experienced writer can use a number of methods to combine all of these ideas into longer, smoother-reading sentences. Carefully review the guidelines for combining sentences in the handbook for explanations and examples of eight basic methods of combining. (Refer to "Sentence, Combining" in the index to find this information.) You may already use many of these methods naturally and effortlessly in your own writing; the others will become part of your toolbox of writing skills with time and practice.

APPLY: Combine the information in sentences one through six above in the four different ways indicated below. (Refer to the section on sentence combining in the handbook for models.) You do not have to include every detail of information in your combined sentences. Also add or change words as necessary.

1. (Use a series to combine three or more similar ideas.)

2. (Use a relative pronoun—*who, whose, that, which*—to introduce a less important idea.)

3. (Use an introductory phrase or clause for the less important idea.)

4. (Use a participial phrase—*ing* or *ed* phrase—at the beginning or end of a sentence.)

Combining Simple Ideas

Remember that combining simple ideas allows you to say much more in your sentences—to express several basic ideas that work together in effective and thoughtful ways. What you pay for in length in combined sentences, you get back in clear thinking and focus. (Think about it.)

PRACTICE: Here's a subject nearly anyone can write about: scars. Find a scar somewhere on your body. If you've had a cushy life and can't find a scar, try a freckle or a mole. Can't find even a single blemish? Okay. Write about your nose, or whatever. Write three very short sentences.

Example: My scar is on my eyebrow. It came from chicken pox. It may never go away.

Write your sentences here:

1. ....

2. ....

3. ....

COMBINE: Choose one of the methods of combining sentences listed in your handbook, perhaps a method you've never worked with before. (Refer to "Sentence, Combining" in the index.) You might, for instance, use a relative pronoun. Now combine your three sentences into one effective sentence:

Example: The scar on my eyebrow, WHICH came from chicken pox, may never go away.
(combined with a relative pronoun)

Write your sentence here: ....

WRITE: Here is an entire paragraph about a scar. All the ideas are broken down into their smallest parts. Put the ideas together into five or six logical and clearly written sentences that together comprise one clear paragraph. (Put your work on your own paper.)

My scar is on my knee. It came from a go-cart accident. I was a girl when the accident happened. The go-cart didn't have any brakes. I was riding in circles on a parking lot. The parking lot was at a church. I started to spin out. I was spinning out around a sharp corner. I scraped my tennis shoes on the pavement. I did that so I could stop. My feet jammed up under me. My feet flipped me forward. I was lying there on the go-cart. For a moment, my left knee was scraping on the blacktop. Later, I examined the scrape. The scrape had a shape. The shape happened to look like a heart. It was perfectly shaped. When I saw the heart, I understood immediately. I understood it had some deep, deep meaning.

I'm Going Through a Phrase

Often you can combine two sentences by making one of them an introductory phrase or clause. That is, information from one sentence is used to introduce the information in the other.

Sentences: I sat down to write.
I put on a B. B. King cassette first.

Combined: After putting on a B. B. King cassette, I sat down to write.

COMBINE: Now you try it. Combine the following sets of sentences by making introductory phrases or clauses. Use the frameworks provided as a guide.

1. The phone rang for the fourth time. My mom threw a shoe at it.

   As the ...., my mom

   ....

2. The storm ripped up trees and phone lines. It made its way slowly across southern Oklahoma.

   Ripping ....,

   the storm ....

3. I swam at Baxter's. I got the blues and French-braided my hair.

   After swimming ...., I got

   ....

4. My parents had reservations about the trip. They let me go.

   Despite their ...., my

   ....

5. The camping trip was cold. It was rainy. It was muddy. We had a great time on our trip.

   Although it was ...., ...,

   ...., we ....

Prepositional, participial, infinitive, and appositive phrases can all be used to combine sentences. (Refer to "Sentence, Combining" and "Phrase" in the handbook index for more information.) Combine the following sets of simple sentences, using the type of phrase indicated. (The phrase can come at the beginning, in the middle, or at the end of the main sentence.)

1. The car came screeching to a rubber-burning halt. It halted in front of the gas station. *(prepositional phrase)*

   The car came screeching to a rubber-burning halt <u>in front of the gas station</u>.

2. Many motorists sped past the two-car accident without stopping. They left the two victims stranded on the side of the road. *(participial phrase)*

3. Herman put a fence around his garden. He wanted to stop the rabbits from eating his vegetables. *(infinitive phrase)*

4. My aunt Deb is the woman waving her arm off. She's the only relative who came to meet me at the airport. *(appositive phrase)*

5. Riley ran powerfully and recklessly. He chased the bus down the street. *(participial phrase)*

SHARE: Compare your work. Remember that sentence combining always comes down to a writer's own personal choices. There is more than one way to combine simple sentences.

Compounding Ideas

READ: As you know, a compound sentence contains two independent clauses (simple sentences) of equal importance. The two independent clauses in a compound sentence may be joined by a semicolon, or a comma and a coordinate conjunction. The specific coordinating conjunction to use depends on the relationship of the two clauses to each other. (See the examples below.)

1. Kangaroos roam in groups called "mobs"; the leader is known as "the old man." (two independent clauses connected by a semicolon)

2. He must keep the young bucks in order, and he often does so with boxing maneuvers. (two clauses connected by a comma and a conjunction that adds equal ideas)

3. The kangaroo can defend himself by boxing, or he can deliver vicious kicks with his hind legs. (clauses connected by a comma and a conjunction that presents a choice)

4. His tail is strong enough to support his body, so the kangaroo can freely use his arms and legs to punch and kick. (clauses connected by a comma and a conjunction that shows a result)

5. A careless hound may be fast enough to corner a kangaroo, but he will be most unhappy at the painful result. (clauses connected by a comma and a conjunction that shows a contrast)

REACT: All of the following compound sentences use "and" as the coordinating conjunction. To communicate the exact relationship between the two independent ideas, choose a different coordinating conjunction where needed. Revise each sentence accordingly. *Note:* If the relationship in any of the sentences is "ideas added together," you may choose to leave the "and" or to drop it and use a semicolon. (Use the following coordinating conjunctions: *and, but, or, nor, for, yet, so.*)

1. A careless circus trainer once allowed a boxing kangaroo to escape in Tokyo, Japan, ~~and~~ *so* the gloved animal set off on a tour of the city. *(show a result)*

2. Several police cars and pedestrians set off in hot pursuit, and the chase was harder than they could have imagined. *(show a contrast)*

3. The kangaroo, named Fuji, could run away from his opponents at speeds of up to 40 miles per hour, and he could turn and put up a spirited defense with his boxing gloves. *(present a choice)*

4. Fuji was downing his opponents with well-placed punches, and a policeman finally put a judo submission hold on him. *(show a contrast)*

5. In another kangaroo tale, a man was driving across part of Australia, and he accidentally knocked down a large kangaroo. *(show ideas added together)*

6. The kangaroo lay limp on the ground, and the motorist assumed it was dead. *(show a result)*

7. The traveler wanted an interesting picture for his photo album, and he decided to dress the animal in his coat. *(show a result)*

8. Having propped the dapper-looking hopper against a tree, the man readied his camera, and he was soon startled by the kangaroo's waking and bounding off, still wearing the coat. *(show a contrast)*

REACT: You can also combine two sentences by using a compound verb. (Refer to "Compound, Predicate" in the handbook index for more information.)

1. I watched a young woman bungee-jump into a deep gorge. I immediately knew she was much braver than I was.

   I watched a young woman bungee-jump into a deep gorge and immediately knew she was much braver than I was.

2. The California coastline boasts rugged, majestic cliffs. It also offers beautiful, sun-washed beaches.

3. My uncle Joe, who lives in northern Minnesota, has never traveled by train. He has also never flown on an airplane.

4. We'll play volleyball all morning. Then we'll take a siesta during the afternoon.

Creating Complex Sentences 1

To join two ideas that are not equal in importance, use a **complex sentence**. A complex sentence contains one independent clause (the main idea) and one or more dependent, or subordinate, clauses (secondary ideas). Subordinate clauses are called adverb clauses when they begin with a subordinate conjunction. Common subordinate conjunctions include *when, where, since, although, before, after, until, because, unless, if,* and *while*. Note the following complex sentence containing an independent clause (boldfaced) and an adverb clause (italicized) beginning with a subordinate conjunction (circled).

(Before) *you set out on that hi-tech mountain bike,* **please think a little bit about the history of biking.**

COMBINE: Seven sets of simple sentences follow. Combine each set into two different complex sentences using the subordinate conjunctions listed above. An asterisk (*) is printed after the more important idea in the first few sets. Remember that a subordinate conjunction introduces the dependent or secondary idea. (The first one has been done for you.)

1. John Dunlop had a problem.* His young son was always falling off his tricycle.

   A. John Dunlop had a problem **because** his young son was always falling off his tricycle.

   B. **Since** his young son was always falling off his tricycle, John Dunlop had a problem.

2. John Dunlop lived in Belfast, Ireland.* The streets in Belfast were made of rough cobblestone.

   A. ....

   ....

   B. ....

   ....

3. Nothing could be done about the rough streets. The tricycle had to be improved.*

   A. ....

   ....

   B. ....

   ....

4. John Dunlop carefully considered the problem. He decided to replace the tricycle's old wheels with air-filled tubes.

A ....

....

B. ....

....

5. Air-filled tires were used in 1888 by bicycle racers. Most people still laughed at the idea of "riding on air."

A. ....

....

B. ....

....

6. The air-filled tire was later used successfully on carriages. People stopped laughing.

A. ....

....

B. ....

....

7. Today's cars ride on air-filled tires. A little boy once had a problem riding his tricycle on the rough streets of Belfast, Ireland.

A. ....

....

B. ....

....

Creating Complex Sentences 2

An adjective clause in a complex sentence begins with a **relative pronoun**—*who*, *whom*, *whose*, *which*, *what*, or *that*. Adjective clauses describe a noun in the independent (main) clause. Put more simply, they act like pointers. Relative pronouns say, "Hey, this group of words beginning with *who, whose, which,* or *that* describes that noun." (See the underlined adjective clauses in the following complex sentences.)

The train that derailed in northern Wisconsin spilled hundreds of gallons of benzine.

Many residents, who were in danger of being poisoned, had to be evacuated.

COMBINE: Combine the following sentences using adjective clauses. In each case, we've given you a framework to help you along, but we haven't put in the commas. You'll have to decide for yourself whether or not the adjective clauses need to be set off with commas. (Refer to "Clause, Restrictive, nonrestrictive" in the handbook index for help.)

1. Panic attack sufferers feel threatened or out of control. They say that nothing in particular causes the sensation.

.... who ....

.... feel ....

2. The increase in heart rate and blood pressure can come on very suddenly. These two symptoms characterize panic attacks.

The increase .... that characterizes

....

3. Doctors have been studying the phenomenon. They say that increased lactate, a natural chemical in the blood, can bring on panic attacks.

.... who .... say

....

4. But no one really knows for sure what brings on the attacks. The attacks may cause shortness of breath and a crushing feeling of doom.

But .... which

....

Combining in Review

WRITE: Use at least ten of the facts listed below in five (or fewer) sentences. Obviously, you'll have to do some sentence combining in order to succeed. How you combine ideas is entirely up to you, but try to vary the combining methods you use. (Refer to "Sentence, Combining" in the handbook index if you need help.) One sample sentence is done for you.

Ravens

- are the most intelligent type of bird
- like to do midair acrobatics while playing
- have fantastic memories
- have a wingspan of four feet
- mate for life
- live in constant, stable flocks
- are related to crows

- are very playful
- are related to jays and magpies
- can recognize a gun from a great distance
- make great pets
- can learn to count
- know 60 different birdcalls of their own
- can remember more than 1,000 hiding places for food

1. Ravens must have fantastic memories if they can remember more than 1,000 hiding places for food.

2. ....
....

3. ....
....

4. ....
....

5. ....
....

extend Use all 14 facts in as few sentences as possible. (Make a contest out of this activity and see who can say the most in the fewest sentences.)

Writing in Rhythm

An effective way to present equal ideas in your writing is to use **parallel structure**. When you use parallel structure, you put similar ideas in a similar form. This allows you to leave out unnecessary words and makes your thoughts easier to follow. By using parallel structure, you can make your writing *more compact*, *more rhythmic*, and *more energetic*. Look at the italicized words in the sentence above to see parallel structure in action. (Refer to "Parallel structure" in the handbook index for more information.)

REACT: Combine each pair of sentences below into one sentence by using parallel structure. Remember, each idea must be written in the same way, using the same kinds of words. (The first one is done for you.)

1. My brother's room is full of half-eaten sandwiches.
It also has lots of dirty socks and *Mad* magazines.

My brother's room is full of half-eaten sandwiches, dirty socks, and <u>Mad</u> magazines.

2. Kareem wants to go to college and then become a volunteer medic.
He hopes to work in the African sub-Sahara.

....

....

3. To become a top mechanic, you have to acquire the necessary knowledge.
You must also develop the proper skills and get hands-on experience.

....

....

4. When she began to pick up the room, the baby-sitter found a broken kite and a cardinal feather. She also found a collection of bottle caps.

....

....

5. The once-shy 12-year-old danced with his friends.
He was impressing them with his talent.
(One of the two verbs in these sentences will have to be changed so the two are parallel.)

....

....

Imitating Models

Below you will find a variety of sentences to study, imitate, and revise. The more you play with sentences like these, the more secure you will feel when you try to invent or revise your own.

Slowly read each of these sentences to yourself. Then read them out loud to a listener. During your reading aloud, use the word "comma" to mark the punctuation. (The main subject and verb are italicized to help you better understand the structure of each sentence.)

Psst! All of the sections in your handbook listed under "Sentence" in the index will help you expand your understanding of sentence structure for this activity.

WRITE: Imitate the style and form of five of the sentences below (and on the next page) as exactly as you can while saying something about topics of your own choosing. (Think of television programs, your neighborhood, a sporting event, or whatever.) One sample sentence is provided.

1. *The foal trots* forward a few steps, then *halts*, trembling, her furry ears flicking back and forth.

   — Jane Smiley

   The child shuffles forward a few steps, then hesitates, listening, her sticky fingers tapping nervously on her lips.

2. *This amounted* to nothing better than the waving of the white flag, surrender, armistice, failure, humiliation.

   — William Saroyan

3. *To be* an American and unable to play baseball *is* comparable to being a Polynesian and unable to swim.

   — John Cheever

4. Eyes watching, horns straight forward, *the bull looked* at him, watching.

> — Ernest Hemingway

5. Now and then *she came* in with a shallow box full of newly hatched chickens, abject dabs of wet fluff, *and put* them on a table in her bedroom where she might tend them carefully on their first day.

> — Katherine Anne Porter

6. *She seemed* to stare endlessly outward and down, in the face of the wind more piercing than any she had felt on earth, feeling herself propelled with speed into a kingdom where nothing could help her, neither her pride, nor her courage, nor her glorious wickedness.

> — James Baldwin

7. On his magic throat there *swelled* a breaking *sorrow*, a terrible, stirring sorrow that made their spines go cold with joy.

> — Kay Boyle

extend   Identify one of your partner's sentences that works very well. Study the form as well as the content. Then explain to your partner why you chose the sentence.

Getting It Right

Writing is a bit like decorating a room. You start with white walls and bare floors and then begin to add the contents. Furniture determines what kind of room it will be; pictures and posters personalize the room. Curtains let in a certain amount of light and so on. You keep adding, subtracting, and rearranging the features until the room has the right look and feel to it. The same holds true for writing. You must add and subtract details until your work looks and feels just right.

READ: Study the "Primer Style" section in your handbook. (Refer to "Writing with style, Ailments of style" in the index.) Then read the paragraph below and do whatever subtracting, rearranging, or combining is necessary to produce writing that looks and sounds better than the original sample. After you finish your revision, show it to a classmate and ask for feedback.

(1) Our school's cafeteria is used for voting. (2) People come there to vote on Election Day. (3) The direction signs to get to the cafeteria are bad. (4) People get lost in the halls. (5) They wander into our classrooms. (6) They get upset with us. (7) It's not our fault! (8) They need better directions.

extend Here's a special challenge: Write a primer-style paragraph about any subject (maybe about a memorable store owner) to exchange with a classmate. Give your classmate's paragraph your personal touch by adding, cutting, and combining details until you feel the writing suits your taste.

Writing Metaphorically

One of the most important skills a writer can develop is the ability to create mental images or word pictures. These mental images are "rings" that help the reader swing from one idea to the next. There are several types of "rings"—metaphor, simile, analogy, specific details, and so on. This activity focuses on writing with metaphors and similes.

REACT: Rewrite the following sentences, using metaphors or similes to create interesting mental pictures that show rather than tell. (See "Metaphor" and "Simile" in your handbook index for more examples.)

1. The elephant was old.
   The skin on the elephant's back sagged like an oversized, hand-me-down gray sweater.

2. My grandmother's eyes saw everything.

3. Tuna-fish casserole is not my favorite meal.

4. The first day of school makes me nervous.

5. My brother loves to wear baggy pants, old tennis shoes, and torn T-shirts.

6. The roller coaster was scary.

7. Ms. Peterson's voice is powerful.

WRITE: List three telling sentences about school life and exchange them with a classmate. Change your partner's examples into showing sentences, using metaphors or similes. Compare the results.

Refining:
Working with Words

All the Right Parts

From elementary school onward, you have probably been expected to know the eight basic parts of speech. Can you name them?

Here's a review: noun, pronoun, adjective, verb, adverb, preposition, conjunction, interjection. Even if you couldn't remember all eight without a prompt, you can be sure that you've been using all of them in your everyday conversation and writing.

REVIEW: Before you go on with the rest of this workshop, review the definitions of each part of speech by looking up "Parts of speech" in the index of the handbook. Pay especially close attention to any definition that is new or unfamiliar to you.

RESPOND: All eight parts of speech are contained in the following sentence. Some of them appear several times. Can you identify the part of speech of each word as it is used in the sentence?

> Hey, a CD player and some good speakers at the foot of my bed always clear my head when I flop down with my homework after supper.

Here is a list of the eight parts of speech. Place each word from the sentence after the appropriate name:

Noun:

Pronoun:

Verb:

Adjective:

Adverb:

Preposition:

Conjunction:

Interjection:

WRITE: Now compose your own sentence that contains all eight parts of speech. (Work on this with a partner if your teacher allows it.) Then exchange your sentence with a classmate (or another team) and find the parts of speech in each other's work.

inside
info →

Does it really matter whether you know the eight basic parts of speech? Well, knowing them won't directly improve your writing. But almost any discussion about writing style, organization, or logic will sooner or later come around to one or more of the parts of speech. Similarly, knowing the names of the muscles won't directly affect your running and jumping. But as soon as you want to get in shape or do some bodybuilding, you may very well find yourself talking about pectorals, deltoids, biceps, and abdominals.

Painting Pictures

Writing is the process of transferring what is in your mind to your reader's mind. Suppose in your mind you see a majestic moose, with head held high, crashing out of a forest of tall pine trees.

Now suppose you write, "The animal came out of the woods." How clearly do you think you would have communicated your original thought, or image, to the reader? Obviously, not very clearly. By using **specific words**, you can create a **specific word picture** for your reader.

Look at the examples below. Notice that the nouns in the blanks move from very general at the top to very specific at the bottom. By using specific nouns in your writing, you will make it easier for the reader to "see" the picture you have in your mind.

person	place	thing	idea

SPECIFY: Now think of three nouns for each of the categories below. Each word you add must be more specific than the one before (as in the example above).

person	place	thing	idea

REWRITE: Revise each of the following sentences twice. Create a clearer picture each time by substituting a more specific noun for each underlined word. In other words, sentence B should be more specific than sentence A. (See the example below.) Also, feel free to add or change other words as necessary to create a better sentence.

Example: The <u>car</u> went past the <u>building</u>.

A. The foreign car went past the government building.

B. The Toyota went past the White House.

1. The book is in the room.

A ....

B. ....

2. The singer sang the song.

A ....

B. ....

3. A student brought me a paper.

A. ....

B. ....

4. The player was given an award.

A. ....

B. ....

5. A family member had an injury.

A. ....

B. ....

6. A local business is having a sale.

A. ....

B. ....

extend Look through some of your recent writings and see if any could be improved by using more specific nouns.

Vive la vivid verb!

Like nouns, verbs can be too general to create a vivid word picture for the reader. For example, the verb "looked" does not say the same thing to the reader as "stared, glared, glanced, peeked," or "inspected." Likewise, the sentence "John *went* down the stairs" doesn't provide a very vivid picture. The reader doesn't know "how" John went or "how he felt." The picture is too general.

If, on the other hand, you were to write, "John *tiptoed* down the stairs" or "John *charged* down the stairs," the reader would be able to see John move and imagine how he felt.

This explains why you should use vivid verbs whenever you are describing important action. Vivid verbs make writing come alive for readers, helping them to feel as well as see the action.

Guidelines for Revising Verbs

● Whenever possible, use a verb that is strong enough to stand alone without the help of an adverb.

Verb and adverb: Joan **sat down** on the sofa.

A single vivid verb: Joan **plopped** on the sofa.

● Use active rather than passive verbs. (Use passive verbs only if you want to "play down" who is doing or performing the action in the sentence.)

Passive verb: The football **was clutched** by Jocko.

Active verb: Jocko **clutched** the football.

● Avoid overusing the "to be" verbs (*is, are, were, am, . . .*). Also avoid overusing *would, could,* or *should*. Often a better verb can be made from another word in the same sentence.

A "to be" verb: Barry **is** someone who dreams about acting.

A stronger verb: Barry **dreams** about acting.

● Use verbs that show rather than tell.

A verb that tells: Greta **is** very tall.

A verb that shows: Greta **towers** over the other girls.

REVISE: In each of the following sentences, substitute one vivid verb for the verb and adverb in parentheses. Before you begin, look up the topics listed under "Verbs, vivid" in the index of your handbook.

1. John (*quickly went*) _____ dashed _____ across the road.

2. Sarah (*talked briefly*) .... with her neighbor.

3. Ming (*quickly read*) .... the assignment.

4. Rosa (*carefully read*) .... the assignment.

5. Sam (*looked briefly*) .... out the window.

6. Emil (*looked blankly*) .... out the window.

REVISE: In the paragraph below, substitute a vivid verb for each verb in parentheses that you feel needs improving. (*Note:* Do not replace any verb you feel is vivid enough already. Simply leave those lines blank.)

I (*had*) .... my share of injuries when I was little. Once I was playing cars and was (*moving*) .... right along when I (*fell*) .... over my steering wheel—which was really my blanket—and (*cut*) .... my chin open on the rocking chair. My dad had to (*take*) .... me to the doctor to get stitches. Another time, when I was about four years old, everyone was (*sitting*) .... on the porch, and I was (*resting*) .... in the living room alone. For some reason I was (*looking*) .... underneath the couch, and I (*saw*) .... a strange object. Curiosity overcame me, and I (*got*) .... the object only to discover too late that it was a large fishing hook, and it was (*cutting*) .... fiercely into my thumb. I (*called loudly*) .... , and my mom came (*running* .... She tried to (*take*) .... it out, but only succeeded in (*moving*) .... it in farther. Our neighbor (*took*) .... me to the doctor, and the doctor had to (*cut*) .... it out. When I got home, my brother (*was upset*) .... because I let the doctor throw the fishhook away. So much for brotherly sympathy.

inside info → Remember: Use vivid verbs whenever they will add to the impact of your writing. Just don't overdo it!

Add more details!

If you're like most of us, you have been told at one time or another to "add more color, more detail" to your writing. And, like most of us, you probably went back to your work and did just that—added as many colorful adjectives as you could.

Or maybe you've been told that your adjectives are too general or overused. In either case, the following activity should help. Look carefully at the two CAUTIONS before you begin.

CAUTION #1: **Avoid gray, lifeless, overused adjectives:**

okay	boring	good	small	weird
awesome	cool	great	terrific	bad
cute	interesting	big	different	funny
dumb	neat	fine	nice	fun

CAUTION #2: **Don't use too many adjectives in your writing or your best ones won't stand out.** For example, read this sentence: "A tall, shocking column of thick, yellow smoke marked the exact spot where the illegal drug lab blew up." Doesn't that sound a bit overdone? Take out about half the adjectives and notice the improvement: "A column of thick, yellow smoke marked the spot where the illegal drug lab blew up."

REVISE: Replace the underlined adjectives with more colorful, vivid ones. In the process, revise any noun or verb that is not as strong as it could be.

1. Our teacher is <u>nice</u>. **Revised:** Our science teacher is patient and understanding.

2. The band was <u>good</u>. **Revised:** ....

....

3. It was a <u>warm</u> day. **Revised:** ....

....

4. The pizza was <u>good</u>. **Revised:** ....

....

5. The <u>messy</u> room needed cleaning. **Revised:** ....

....

6. The <u>boring</u> demonstration was part of our <u>boring</u> class. **Revised:** ....

....

CLARIFY: In the sentences below, remove or replace any adjectives that clutter rather than clarify.

1. The young, thin, half-starved man stumbled out of the thick, lush, green underbrush and into the small, isolated mountain village.

....

....

2. The first bright rays of the early morning sun invaded the darkness and serenity of our lake cottage about the same time the noisy, obnoxious, uninvited chirping of the local bird population invaded the silence.

....

....

3. A large, towering, giant oak tree stood in the exact center of our small front lawn, shading our entire home from the hot, blistering afternoon sun.

....

....

4. The dry, yellow, sun-bleached grass snapped and crunched under our feet, leaving an eerie, unearthly trail of footprints behind us.

....

....

**extend** Review something you have written recently for the use of adjectives. Add or cut modifiers as necessary.

Let's Play Alphabet Talk

I turned on a cable-TV network the other day and here were these comedians playing a dialogue game that had the audience rolling. I thought, "Hey! This would be good for students who have trouble writing natural-sounding dialogue." You can limber up your dialogue-writing skills with a game that will be equally fun whether you play it at school or at home.

The Game

You need two people to play "alphabet talk." First you choose a topic or situation. Then you choose a letter of the alphabet, say "G," and begin a conversation. But the first speaker has to make a comment starting with "G." The other has to make a response starting with "H." The first one answers back starting with "I," and so on, around the alphabet until you come back to "G." You can do this out loud, thinking quickly on your feet, or you can write your dialogue, passing a paper back and forth.

Example: We agree that the situation will be two people arguing over a silver dollar they found on the street. The starting letter is "B." Here's how the dialogue might go:

She: **B**efore you pick that up, consider who saw it first.

He: **C**onsider, instead, who needs it most.

She: **D**o you presume to know my needs?

He: **E**verybody has a need for a pleasant surprise now and then. It would surprise me if you would take your foot off the thing and let me have it.

She: **F**or a small sum, maybe I would.

He: **G**reed runs in some families, I'm told.

She: **H**orsefeathers. It's individuals who are greedy. Even some otherwise attractive individuals.

He: **I** wonder who you might be referring to.

She: **J**ust think about it.

TALK: Well, you get the picture—or the sound, anyway. Now try an "alphabet talk" of your own. The faster you go, the more fun it is.

Suggested topics and situations:

● Two kids argue about who has to wash the dog.

● At 35,000 feet a pilot and a flight attendant discuss how to tell the passengers that ground control has just reported a possible bomb on board.

● Behind a circus tent, a clown tries to talk a reluctant teenager into running away from home.

● Two students of different races, the last to leave a locker room, discover that despite their differences, they have a lot in common.

● (Make up a situation of your own.)

Wordsmithing

READ: Read and enjoy the following passage describing the grounds surrounding a deserted home known as the Clark Mansion. (Reprinted from *Good Old Boy* by Willie Morris.)

That house seemed to cast an unwholesome influence over the very countryside that surrounded it, for there were acres and acres . . . of tall dull trees more dead than alive, their branches heavy with Spanish moss, and everywhere a dense undergrowth of thorny vines and grasses infested, no doubt, with rattlers and copperheads. A narrow dirt road wound its way two miles through this forbidden terrain to the house. The trees themselves were twisted into grotesque shapes none more so than the prodigious oak which had grown into the roof; from the distance the tree resembled a bloated and silent old owl. Behind the house and the tree, some fifty yards away, was the Yazoo River: a living presence with its murky currents and eddies and its fierce rhythmic roar . . .

REACT: According to the topic sentence in this passage, the house "cast an unwholesome influence" on the surroundings. Carefully review the passage and underline five phrases that do, in fact, suggest that the Clark Mansion had a negative influence. Share your results.

WRITE: Describe a specific place or object, using the model paragraph as your guide. Your topic sentence should identify a dominant feeling about the subject of your writing. Work four or five descriptive words or phrases into the body of your writing to support your topic sentence. (Use your own paper.)

inside info → Use descriptive words selectively in your writing, only when it seems important or natural to do so. Too many descriptive words, piled one on top of another, make writing sound forced and artificial.

Keep It Simple

Do you suffer from the "more-is-better" syndrome? Do you have an irresistible urge to fill your writing with unnecessary words and phrases? It's a problem of running off at the pen, generally. The cure? Cut or simplify all that is redundant, unnecessary, or wordy.

EDIT: Study the following paragraph. It contains a number of unnecessary words and phrases. Without these words, the paragraph will be cleaner and crisper. Go through the paragraph and place brackets around as many unnecessary words as you can find. (Some of the unnecessary words have already been identified for you.)

Psst! For further information on redundancy, excessive adjectives, slang, jargon, or deadwood, read the section called "Common Ailments of Style." (Refer to "Style, Ailments" in the index.) Also refer to "Writing Natural Sentences." (See "Sentence, Writing effectively" in the handbook index to find this information.)

My mother, a native New Yorker [who has lived in New York her whole life,] recently went [to Africa] on an African safari, [which some people thought was an odd trip for an elderly woman]. I don't know when or how the idea was first introduced to her, but as soon as she heard about the safari trip, she began reading everything she could get her hands on about Africa. The safari, which was organized last year, was composed of fifteen senior citizens, none of whom had ever heard of a zebu and most of whom thought the Watusi was only a 1960's dance. Needless to say, my mother and her fellow senior citizen explorers were very impressed with the wealth of natural beauty and living animal life on the African plains and in the jungles. Consequently, they returned from their African journey with memories of a culture and of a wilderness that will remain with them always.

extend Select something you have recently written. Exchange it for a classmate's paper and place brackets around any obvious wordiness, redundancy, excessive adjectives, slang, jargon, or deadwood in your partner's work.

Refining: Editing

Editing Checklist

Have you ever used a shopping or study list? Isn't it helpful to have your thoughts organized? The following checklist should help you each time you review and edit your writing. You might think of it as a "chopping" list, but it's really more: chopping, connecting, rearranging, polishing, . . .

1. Read your final draft aloud to test it for sense and sound. Better yet, have someone read it aloud to you. Listen carefully as he or she reads. Your writing should read smoothly and naturally. If it doesn't, you have more editing to do.

2. Does each sentence express a complete thought? Does each paragraph have an over all point or purpose?

3. Have you used different sentence types and lengths? Are any sentences too long and rambling? Do you use too many short, choppy sentences?

4. Have you used a variety of sentence beginnings? Watch out for too many sentences that begin with the same pronoun or article (*I, My, The,* etc.).

5. Check each simple sentence for effective use of modifiers, especially prepositional phrases, participial phrases, and appositives. Have you punctuated these modifiers correctly?

6. Check your compound sentences. Do they contain two equal ideas, and is the logical relationship between the two ideas expressed by the proper conjunction (*and* versus *but* versus *or* . . .)?

7. What about your complex sentences? Have you used subordination effectively? Does the independent clause contain the most important idea? Are less important ideas contained in dependent clauses?

8. Make sure your writing is concise and to the point. Have you omitted jargon, slang, redundancies, and other forms of wordiness?

9. Is your writing fresh and original? Have you avoided overused words and phrases? If not, substitute nouns, verbs, and adjectives that are specific, vivid, and colorful.

10. Replace any words or phrases that may be awkward, confusing, or misleading.

Agreement of Subject and Verb

EDIT: Locate and underline the subjects in the paragraph below; then circle the correct verb forms (singular or plural). See the "Agreement of Subject and Verb" section in your handbook for additional information. (Refer to "Agreement, Subject/verb" in the index for this information.)

1   <u>Malorie</u> and <u>Emma</u> (are/is) best friends. They (have/has) known each other since

2   they attended nursery school together. Now that they (are/is) older, they know that

3   friendships like theirs (are/is) dependent upon trust and reliability. As trust and

4   reliability (grow/grows), the friendship (become/becomes) stronger. All of their friends

5   (wonder/wonders) how two people who are so different could remain friends for so long.

6   Malorie says each of them (complements/complement) the other; they go together like

7   cookies and milk. Emma thinks they share important basic beliefs; they may look

8   different, but their values (is/are) the same. She also believes their friendship is not that

9   unusual. She (point/points) to several of their friends who also (share/shares) long-term

10   friendships. Everyone, says Emma, (is/are) capable of having a long-term friendship; you

11   just have to open your heart. Neither Malorie nor Emma (enjoys/enjoy) simply collecting

12   acquaintances. Friends (are/is) good, and good friends (is/are) even better.

An inverted sentence is one in which the true subject comes after the verb (instead of before). Inverted sentences are often used so that the important idea falls at the end of the sentence. Just be certain that the verb agrees in number with the subject. Underline the subject for each set of verbs below; then select the verb that agrees in number with the subject. Write your answer on the blank provided.

.... _were_ .... **1.** In the library (were/was) ten biology <u>students</u> preparing for an exam.

.... **2.** (Is/Are) either of the boys attending the basketball game tonight?

.... **3.** In our class (is/are) three students who will be studying in Spain next summer.

.... **4.** (Has/Have) your mother or father given you permission to take driver's education this summer?

Pronoun/Antecedent Agreement

Just as subjects must agree in number and person with their verbs, **pronouns** must agree in number, person, and gender with their **antecedents**. An antecedent is the word that a pronoun refers to or replaces. We'll use the following sentence to explain how all of this works:

Shel Novotny lost *his* pet tarantula in biology class.

DISCUSSION: In the sample sentence above you will note that *Shel Novotny* and *his* are both italicized. The antecedent in the sentence is *Shel Novotny*; the pronoun *his* refers to Shel Novotny. The pronoun and antecedent agree in number (they are both singular), in person (they are both in the third person), and in gender (they are both masculine). *Psst!* Don't be confused by all of this. Taken as a whole, pronoun/antecedent agreement is not an issue you have to worry too much about when you write. It is only in a few cases that it might cause you problems. And that's the purpose of this workshop: to make you aware of some of the pronoun/antecedent agreement trouble spots.

REVIEW: Review the rules in the handbook for pronoun/antecedent agreement. (Refer to "Agreement, Antecedent/pronoun" in the index.) Using this information as your guide, complete the following sentence starters: (Use these sentences as a starting point for a class discussion about pronoun/antecedent agreement.)

1. Use a singular pronoun to refer to such antecedents as *each, either, neither, one,*

....

....

2. When *a person* or *everyone* is used to refer to both sexes or either sex, you will have to

....

....

3. Two or more antecedents joined by *and* are considered plural; two or more singular antecedents joined by

....

....

extend   Write two original sentences illustrating each of the pronoun/antecedent rules
→   discussed in this workshop.

A Capital Idea

A **fragment** is a group of words used in error as a sentence. A fragment is either a phrase or clause masquerading as a sentence. Remember: A sentence must contain a subject and a verb and present a complete thought. (See "Fragment sentence" in your handbook index for more information and examples.)

EDIT: See how well you do at spotting fragments. Write "S" before each sentence and "F" before each fragment.

Examples:

     S   **1.** America's first amusement parks were built in the 1800's.

     F   **2.** Started in New England and quickly spread across the country. (missing subject)

     3. The first amusement parks started because streetcar companies were charged a high monthly fee for electricity.

     4. Wanted the public to ride streetcars on weekends.

     5. By building an attraction at the end of the streetcar line.

     6. The Fitchburg and Leominster Street Railway Company built Whalom Parkin Lunenburg, Massachusetts, in the late 1890's.

     7. With a picnic grove, dance hall, rides, and games on a 75-acre site.

     8. By 1900 performances of grand opera in Whalom Park's 3,000-seat, open-sided summer theater.

     9. When silent movies attracted big audiences.

     10. Amusement parks all over the country hired silent-movie stars for personal appearances.

     11. Originally, American amusement parks were adult recreation areas.

     12. Streetcar companies soon sold their huge amusement parks to private operators who are still going strong today.

EDIT: Read the paragraph below, looking for fragments as you go. Revise each fragment by adding whatever words are necessary to create a complete sentence.

1   Shortly after the amusement parks were taken over by private businesses,

2   people began complaining about problems. Wanted the parks kept open, but cleaned

3   up. Sometimes the cities bought the parks from their owners. For example,

4   Chattanooga, Tennessee; Green Bay, Wisconsin; Providence, Rhode Island; Findlay,

5   Ohio. Others bought by civic-minded groups or companies to provide good family

6   entertainment and boost their image. For example, the Chamber of Commerce in

7   Jacksonville, Florida, became owner and operator of Boardwalk Beach Amusement

8   Park. Today, most amusement parks owned by private businesses again. Most of

9   these parks pride themselves on their family entertainment and clean surroundings.

10   In addition to rides and games, also offer live entertainment, giant-screened films,

11   and activities for people of all ages. Amusement parks have come a long way in the

12   past 100 years.

Literary Duct Tape

When a writer connects one complete thought with another, using commas as a sort of literary duct tape, that's a **comma splice** error. Thoughts that can stand alone as complete sentences should be punctuated as sentences. They may also be tied together with a comma and a coordinate conjunction (*and*, *but*, *or*, . . .), with a semicolon, or with a semicolon and a conjunctive adverb (*however*, *moreover*, *besides*, . . .) followed by a comma.

EDIT: Below you'll find a variety of comma splice errors. It's your job to fix them by making separate sentences or by tying the thoughts together, using one of the methods mentioned above. (Refer to "Comma, Splice" in your handbook index for help.)

Psst! The more closely related the sentences are to one another, the more likely it is you'll use a semicolon; a semicolon accents this relationship.

1. I was dying to see <u>Wayne's World II</u> on Sunday, my in-laws made us come over to help weed-wack instead.

I was dying to see <u>Wayne's World II</u> on Sunday; however, my in-laws made us come over to help weed-wack instead. (OR: . . . Sunday, but my . . .)

2. My dog Betty hates going to the groomer, she won't get out of the car without a panting, slobbery struggle.

3. Cocaine causes serious psychological problems, it's bad for the heart and nervous system.

4. The national park has picnic tables and shade canopies now, we can go on our picnic on Saturday afternoon.

5. Thanks for finally putting away your clothes, you tracked mud up the stairs when you did it.

....

....

6. There are now environmentally safe household cleaners, they're made out of vegetable by-products.

....

....

7. I could stop at the store on my way home from work, you could shop for me after school.

....

....

8. The red splotches on my legs turned out to be a heat rash, I got it from the crazy space heater that my boss uses at work.

....

....

9. My mom wants Karen to go to medical school, she has applied to the Arizona Institute for Disc Jockeys.

....

....

10. I pulled a muscle in my leg while moving a piano, I couldn't participate in the walkathon this year.

....

....

extend Come up with three comma splice errors that are real tape jobs. Then exchange them with a classmate and go to work "de-ducting" each other's work.

Coasting Along

Run-on sentences are sentences that contain independent clauses joined without adequate punctuation and/or conjunctions. You can correct run-on sentences by using the same methods used to correct comma splices. (Refer to "Run-on sentence" in your handbook index for more information and examples.)

EDIT: Identify each of the following sentences. Write "RO" on the line before each run-on sentence, and insert the punctuation and/or conjunction that will correct it. If the sentence is correct, write "C" on the blank.

_RO_ 1. The thrill of riding a roller coaster is based on fear ⟨, but⟩ accidents on modern roller coasters are extremely rare.

...... 2. Building up suspense is an important part of the illusion of danger; cars clank slowly up an incline before the first rapid plunge downward.

...... 3. A turn near the top of a crest often adds to the sensation of dropping off into space.

...... 4. The illusion of height is another thrill factor so roller coasters are often built some distance away from other tall structures.

...... 5. Roaring under or through something adds to the contrasts in the experience dark tunnels are often used near the beginning of the roller-coaster rides.

...... 6. Roller-coaster cars are built low to the ground this increases the sensation of speed.

...... 7. The addition of railings on the runways increases the illusion of speed the posts flash by and the passengers imagine they are traveling much faster than they really are.

...... 8. Omitting the railings from crests or turns increases the fear of falling off into space.

...... 9. Fear is contagious when someone screams, other passengers catch the emotion.

...... 10. In a few moments, everyone is screaming and either holding on to each other or gripping the safety bar with whitened knuckles.

EDIT: Read the following paragraphs and locate as many run-on sentences as you can. Then correct these errors, using at least three different methods of correction. (See the example in the first sentence below.)

1   The roller coaster was born in Europe; ~~its~~ **Its** ancestor was the ice slide used for

2   centuries as public amusement in Russia. In the late 1700's, a Frenchman

3   transferred the idea from Russia to Paris but the ice slide was impractical in the

4   warmer climate. As a result, he built a ramp of rollers down which his toboggans

5   could slide. For years nobody seemed to remember the invention of the wheel in the

6   1880's, amusement park operators in America were still building artificial coasting

7   courses using rollers on inclined runways.

8   In 1878 Richard Knutsen of Brooklyn took out the first American patent for a

9   roller coaster on wheels; unfortunately, he never built the ride. La Marcus Thompson

10   built the first American roller coaster on wheels at Coney Island in 1884 it was named

11   Thompson's Gravity Pleasure Railway and was an immediate success. Two couples

12   sat facing each other in a cart that was raised by elevator up to a tower the cart then

13   sped down an undulating track, came to a stop, and was raised by elevator for the

14   next ride.

15   The first roller coaster designed on an oval to bring the passengers back to the

16   starting point was opened less than a year after Thompson's Gravity Pleasure

17   Railway. Variations of these first roller coasters followed quickly on the heels of the

18   Coney Island innovators. By the turn of the century, amusement park visitors could

19   thrill to such rides in many locations across the country and the roller coasters

20   became a permanent fixture in America's search for thrills and excitement.

extend Do a 3-minute free writing about a real or imagined roller-coaster ride. (Include plenty of sensory details.) When you finish, study your free-writing material and select a dominant impression. Write a topic sentence and at least five supporting sentences for a paragraph about your ride. As you revise your paragraph, pay special attention to fragment errors, comma splices, and run-on sentences.

Refining: Proofreading

Proofreading Checklist

The following guidelines will help you put the finishing touches on your writing before you share it with your readers. (As you use this checklist, add points of your own to truly make it a "personal" checklist.)

1. Have you spelled all your words correctly? Here are some tips:

   ● Read your writing backward and aloud—one word at a time—so you focus on each word.
   ● Circle each word you are unsure of.
   ● For help, consult the list of commonly misspelled words in your handbook index under "Spelling, Commonly misspelled." (For additional help, check a dictionary.)

2. Does each sentence end with a punctuation mark?

3. Are coordinating conjunctions (*and*, *but*, *or*, *so*, etc.) in compound sentences preceded by a comma? Have you used commas to set off items listed in a series, after introductory clauses, and so on?

4. Have you used apostrophes to show possession or to mark contractions?

5. Is all dialogue or written conversation properly punctuated?

6. Do all sentences and dialogue begin with a capital letter?

7. Have you capitalized the proper names of people, places, and things?

8. Have you misused any of the commonly mixed pairs of words: *there / their / they're; accept / except*? Refer to the section "Using the Right Word" in your handbook or look in the index under "Usage, mixed pairs."

9. Have you used any words, phrases, or sentences that may confuse the reader?

10. Do your subjects and verbs agree in number?

11. Do your pronouns agree with their antecedents?

12. Have you used any sentence fragments, run-ons, or rambling sentences?

13. Have you chosen an appropriate title if one is needed?

14. Is your paper labeled correctly with the author's name and class?

15. Does the form of the writing satisfy the requirements of the assignment?

Test Yourself!

PROOFREAD: Test your skill as a proofreader by working through the paragraphs below. Capitalize each letter that should be capitalized, punctuate or write out each abbreviation, and change punctuation as necessary. (The first few errors have been identified for you.)

1   ℂan you imagine being bored with your life some cool 𝕊aturday afternoon in late

2   autumn? "ⅈ need a change of pace, you'd say to yourself. there's no choice. i must

3   get away from mom and dad from north chicago high school from illinois even from

4   the u s. you'd flip your *newsweek* magazine on the sofa snap off U2's joshua tree,

5   and charge out of the house and down lake avenue toward the museum of science

6   and industry.

7   once you had scrambled up the long stairway between the mammoth pillars and

8   through the tall iron doors, you'd rush toward the room entitled "travels in space and

9   time." there, in the center of the huge room, encircled by a thick purple rope and

10   protected by an armed guard, would stand the silver ship that you had come to use.

11   "u s time machine" (the official title of the newest american invention) would be

12   painted in bold red and blue letters on the side of the capsule.

13   then, just as the armed guard would turn his head, you would dodge behind him,

14   jump the purple rope, jerk open the door of the time capsule, hop in, and lock the

15   latch! quickly, before the guard could react, you'd flip the destination dial to

16   southeastern europe and set the time dial to july 1980 b c you would be reaching

17   for the large red button entitled "instant transport" when you'd hear a strong voice

18   command, keep your hand off that control or i'll shoot! you'd glance up to see the

19   guard's angry eyes glare at you from behind the barrel of his remington automatic.

20   but you'd reach anyway. and as his index finger would begin to squeeze against the

21   trigger, you'd hit the big red button.

extend   When you finish your next piece of writing, exchange papers with a classmate and test yourselves to see how many proofreading errors you can find.

Bunde, Minnesota

PROOFREAD: Review the capitalization, numbers, and abbreviation rules in your handbook. Then proofread the paragraphs on this page for errors. Capitalize each letter that should be capitalized, write out (or use figures for) each number, and punctuate (or write out) each abbreviation.

1   When I was a little boy, **B**unde, **M**innesota, was one of the two cultural centers

2   of my life. **B**unde is a tiny village planted beside ~~minn. highway~~ **Minnesota Highway** 7 about one hundred

3   miles straight west of minneapolis. in fact, the village isn't even a village; the place

4   consists of eight houses, egbert foken's farm, a church, the parsonage, and bunde

5   cemetery. my great-aunt minnie lived in a bulky 2-story house at the west end of

6   bunde. aunt minnie's apple orchard stood between her house and the little square

7   home where grandma ulferts lived with uncle harry, her thirty-five-year-old son.

8   Just North of my grandma lived old mrs. gruising; and north of her lived mrs

9   bode with her forty-year-old son, clarence. before he died, clarence's father, dr. bode,

10   had been the minister at the bunde christian reformed church, which was built next

11   to his home. just east of the church, the bodies of about two hundred prairie settlers

12   rested beside dr. bode under the tall trees and thick sod in the church, cemetery.

13   south of the cemetery, old mrs alberts lived behind a screen of long-haired willow

14   trees and thick honeysuckle—all of which hid her tiny chicken coop and the old,

15   steep-roofed, pale green house that looked like a german cuckoo clock.

16   each day in cars and trucks on minnesota highway seven, hundreds of strangers

17   shot through that little gathering of trees and buildings and gravestones; but i

18   suspect that nearly none realized that what they saw was really the cultural oasis

19   for our farm community.

extend   Bring in a newspaper or magazine article that contains many capitalized words and abbreviations. Share one or two special or unusual examples with a classmate.

Famous First Feats

Commas are an important tool of writing. Omitting a comma or adding an unneeded one in your writing may mislead or confuse your readers. Clear communication depends upon attention to the rules and a good working knowledge of the mechanics of writing.

PROOFREAD Test your skill at using commas by proofreading the paragraph below. Draw a line through any comma that is used incorrectly; add (and circle) any commas needed. (Refer to your handbook for a quick review of comma usage.)

Psst! There are between 15 and 20 errors.

1   The era of the steam railroad began in America on a Saturday morning in

2   August, 1829 in the forests of eastern Pennsylvania. There Horatio Allen a bright,

3   twenty-seven-year-old civil engineer fresh out of Columbia College introduced the

4   country to the "Stourbridge Lion", a seven-ton locomotive. Using the "Lion" as his

5   test vehicle Allen hoped to prove the potential of steam-driven engines as an efficient

6   means of mass transportation. For the test, the locomotive was to be driven across

7   nearby Lackawaxen Creek on a makeshift, wooden, trestle that formed a curve nearly

8   a quarter of a mile long. The many eager onlookers believed that the locomotive

9   known as the "iron monster" would either collapse the trestle or jump the track at

10   the first curve, go over the edge and plunge into the creek thirty feet below. Risking

11   no life but his own Allen, the future president of the Erie Railroad climbed aboard

12   the "Lion", took the throttle, started down the track and made the six-mile run

13   without mishap. Despite the success the "Stourbridge Lion" was declared too heavy

14   for its tracks. It was put into storage, and later used for parts. But the one run had

15   opened the way for future railroads to play a vital role in the settlement, and

16   development of America.

extend

→ Which one comma rule covered above did you not know before today?

You Shall Return

Legend tells us that before going into battle, an ancient Greek warrior went to the oracle at Delphi to find out his future. He was given the following note: "You shall go you shall return never by war shall you perish." In effect, his fate depended on where the missing commas were supposed to be.

You shall go, you shall return, never by war shall you perish. **OR**
You shall go, you shall return never, by war shall you perish.

Chances are that the placement of a comma will never be a matter of life or death for you. Nevertheless, as the above example proves, commas are important. Omitting a comma or incorrectly punctuating a sentence can cause the meaning to be confused.

PROOFREAD:
Review the basic comma rules. (See "Comma" in your handbook index.) Then insert commas where they are needed in the sentences below. Circle each comma you insert. (Please note that some sentences may not need commas.) Finally, after each paragraph, explain why you inserted commas where you did. (In the first example, only two additional commas are needed.)

1 Our world is a wonderfully mysterious place, and all of our questions have not

2 yet been answered. Easter Island may be a small spot on the map of the Pacific

3 Ocean, but it is also an island with a big mystery. Unknown artists carved huge

4 stone statues in a quarry within the crater of the island's old volcano and they

5 somehow moved the statues to their present locations around the island. Over 250

6 statues stand guard on the volcano's slopes and 300 additional statues lie scattered

7 around the slopes of the island's tall cliffs.

Comma Guideline: ....

....

1 Archeologists photographers and an assortment of Easter Island visitors have

2 wondered how the statues were moved from the volcano quarry. The unknown artists

3 used stone tools; they most likely did not have wood for lifting ropes for pulling or

4 wheels for transporting their huge creations. It is not known who carved the huge

5 statues how they were moved or why 80 statues were left half-finished in the quarry.

6 The statues are different heights—the average being between 17 and 26 feet the

7   tallest towering at 72 feet and the shortest measuring 10 feet. They are thought to

8   be modeled after the faces of primitive Polynesians emigrant peoples from Peru or

9   early Caucasian visitors.

Comma Guideline: ....

....

1   Another famous mystery known as Stonehenge is located in England.

2   Stonehenge a collection of carefully placed stones on Salisbury Plain in southern

3   England still fascinates people today. The first builders began their task as early as

4   2500 B.C. Stonehenge's oldest section the cremation cemetery is a series of 56 holes

5   set in a perfect circle 288 feet in diameter. Around 2000 B.C. a second tribe more

6   innovative than the first began moving 82 huge stones from South Wales to

7   Stonehenge.

Comma Guideline: ....

....

1   After the 82 stones arrived at Stonehenge they were placed in two concentric

2   circles. With the help of modern astronomers it is now believed that Stonehenge was

3   used as a calendar to predict the seasons and signal eclipses of the sun and moon.

4   A third group of Stonehenge builders began their work about 1750 B.C. after the

5   major construction of the "calendar" was completed. Although all three groups of

6   primitive people added to Stonehenge they were each from a different culture.

Comma Guideline: ....

....

extend → Grab a pen and paper and write about a mysterious place in your life. What is it? What draws you to it? What is its core—its power? What is its history?

Raising Volcanoes

PROOFREAD: Read the comma rules in your handbook. Then insert commas where they are needed in the sentences below. (Circle each comma you insert.)

1   The story of Paricutin a volcano formed quite recently in Mexico is an interesting

2   one. On February 20 1943 a farmer who had stopped plowing to rest was startled

3   by a column of smoke rising from the middle of his cornfield. Assuming that he must

4   have somehow started a fire he rushed to put it out. He found however that the

5   smoke was coming from a small hole in the ground not from an open fire. The farmer

6   thought for a moment about how to put out this underground fire and then he put

7   a stone over the hole. He checked the hole later and was alarmed by the increased

8   escape of dense black smoke. The farmer recalled feeling the ground tremble recently

9   and he noted that the soil felt hotter than ever under his bare feet. He hurried to

10   town to tell the mayor and to bring some people back with him.

11   When they arrived some time later they saw black smoke billowing from a hole

12   30 feet deep. The first explosion came that very night when a thick column of smoke

13   cinders and ash shot upward for more than a mile. Explosions followed every few

14   seconds; masses of rock which varied in size from that of a walnut to that of a house

15   were hurled continuously into the air. Lava began to flow two days later and the

16   newborn volcano continued to erupt for many months. The lava flows and ash

17   showers obliterated surrounding farms forests and villages. Paricutin the first town

18   destroyed by the eruption gave up its very name to the new "mountain of fire."

extend The next time you write something for science or social studies, check it carefully
for commas. This will help make the paper clearer and easier to follow (and probably result in a higher grade).

Hide-and-Seek

PROOFREAD: Correct any usage errors by drawing a line through the incorrect word and writing the correct form above it. Do not change any word that is correct.

1   Have you ever played hide-and-seek? My brother Casey and I perfected the

2   strategy for winning this game when we were quiet young. We lived in a knew

3   neighborhood wear their were alot of children our age. Every year, starting on

4   Memorial Day and ending on Labor Day, we wood meet our friends under the

5   streetlight in front of Ozzie's house for a late-evening game of hide-and-seek. Than

6   my brother and I wood put our plan into action.

7   The first rule of winning hide-and-seek is "Do not hide." Hiding is the most

8   obvious thing you can do. Rather than using a place such as a garage, a tree, or an

9   empty garbage can, use the dark as your cover. In short, bee obvious. My brother's

10 favorite "hiding" place was an empty birdbath that stood in our neighbor's backyard.

11 Casey would stand in the birdbath, motionless as a statue, until all of the other

12 players were discovered. Then, when the person who was "it" wasn't looking, Casey

13 wood get down and run to home base. It took our friends too years to discover this

14 rule.

15   The second rule of winning hide-and-seek is "Do not seek." This rule would

16 seam to bee the most obvious. If you spend you're time looking for the other players,

17 you will eventually miss someone who will then run to home base while you are gone

18 and free everyone you have captured. Better two hide real close to home bass and

19 wait. Weight until curiosity and fear of the dark haunt the other players; eventually

20 they will creep out of there hiding places. That's you're chance to jump out, tag them,

21 and win the game.

22   The third and final rule of winning this complex game is "Play with a partner."

23   Sum people would understand this too mean "cheat." My brother and I simply called

24   it the buddy system. We would share particularly interesting hiding places, quitely

25   reveal wear other people were hiding, and never, ever tell anyone else about our three

26   rules. We found the buddy system two be the rite system for us; neither of us ever

27   lost a game.

28   Now that we are older and know longer play hide-and-seek, we feel it's only write

29   that we share our secrets with you. After all, what good is knowledge unless you

30   share it?

extend   Find an article in a newspaper or magazine that contains a number of words often confused or misused. Select any five of these words and explain why each is used correctly.

Final Proof: All Together Now

PROOFREAD: Read the essay below. Draw a line through any error you find in capitalization, numbers, abbreviations, punctuation, spelling, and usage and write the correction above it. Add (and circle) punctuation as necessary.

1   My grandmother was born in nineteen hundred in a small village near the

2   italian-swiss boarder. She was the 1st daughter to survive infancy and her parents

3   always treated her like a very special gift. When she was nine years old her parents

4   emigrated to the united states. They hoped the golden shores of america wood offer

5   their daughter the opportunities and advantages so lacking in their own country.

6   During there arduous ocean voyage, one of my grandmother's younger brother's

7   died of dysentery. Her parents were heartbroken however his death became a symbol

8   of Hope and Promise for the entire family. There point of arrival was ellis island, a

9   small island off the shores of new york city. Hear their papers were processed, and

10   doctors examined the entire family, for communicable diseases. The entire family

11   received a clean bill of health and they were allowed to depart for the mainland.

12   In nineteen ten after eight long months the family finally arrived at there

13   destination; San Francisco here they set up house and began there new life in

14   america. San francisco was very good to them. My great grandfather immediately

15   purchased 200 acres of fertile land in what is now known as the napa valley. Here,

16   he planted vineyards and began the slow process of developing a winery the entire

17   family became involved in this endeavor and within five years, there efforts were

18   repaid. The vineyards produced sum of the finest grape harvests in northern calif.

19   By the early nineteen twenties, my grandmothers family owned 1,000 acres of

20   productive vineyards. The days of poverty and hunger were over no longer wood my

21   grandmother wonder about her future.

Practical
Writing

Writing Paragraphs

Writing Paragraphs

The paragraph is the workhorse of school writing. If you are able to write a good paragraph, you can easily learn to write a good essay, report, or essay test answer. Writing a good paragraph is really a matter of solving a problem. You won't always know when you begin writing how you can solve the problem—but you must know what the problem is. You must be able to state clearly at the very beginning what it is you are trying to do, what problem it is you are trying to solve. One way to do this is to use a topic sentence that contains both your subject and your feeling or impression about that subject

READ: Read the opening page in the "Writing Paragraphs" section of your handbook and answer the questions below about paragraphs and topic sentences.

1. What is a paragraph? ....

....

2. When is a paragraph tightly organized? ....

....

READ: Read the information on the "Topic Sentence" in your handbook and use what you've read to complete the statements below.

1. A topic sentence tells what your subject is and ....

....

2. Here is a common formula for writing a topic sentence:

Formula: ....   + ...

....   = ...

Writing Topic Sentences

APPLY the formula for topic sentences to the sentences below by underlining both the subject and dominant impression.

1. <u>Nursing homes</u> can be very <u>depressing</u>.

2. The U2 concert was one of the most unusual I've ever attended.

3. Even though he doesn't try to be, Harold is always in trouble.

4. A weight machine is an incredibly efficient piece of equipment.

5. The old bank building on the corner is now in shambles.

6. The river that runs through the park is badly polluted.

7. Flying a kite is not as easy as it seems.

COMPLETE the sentences below with words or phrases that make each a good topic sentence.

1. The first day of school is often _____ **filled with surprises** _____ .

2. The park where we spend our spare time is _____ .

3. My new _____ is a real _____ .

4. Learning how to _____ is not _____ .

5. My _____ is always _____ .

6. One thing I believe _____ .

WRITE a topic sentence for each of the subjects listed below. Narrow the subject to a topic that is suitable for a paragraph. Be sure to include a clear description of both your subject and dominant impression, but also try to make each sentence interesting.

1. (a near accident) Every time I go down the road to the park, I see the skid marks we accidentally left

there last summer.

2. (the school library)

3. (a game)

4. (an old friend)

5. (your choice of topics)

CHOOSE one of the topics above and list two or three details about that topic.

Topic Sentence:

Detail 1.

Detail 2.

Detail 3.

Creating Effective Topic Sentences

As you may have guessed by now, a good topic sentence is more than a mere statement of subject and dominant impression—it is also a good sentence. It is a sentence that creates a sense of interest, wonder, or even excitement in the reader.

READ each topic sentence below carefully and rewrite those topic sentences that lack a clear subject or a dominant impression. Also rewrite those topic sentences that aren't worded well enough to create interest in the paragraph.

1. My grandmother is very active.

   Even though my grandmother is over 80, she is constantly on the go.

2. I remember one certain person from eighth grade.

3. My uncle Ervin was a very memorable person.

4. The first time I saw my new eighth-grade English teacher, I thought I'd die.

5. An early summer storm turned our campout into a real adventure.

6. I remember my dog Dutchess.

7. I'll never forget Jeff Johnson—he was like a brother to me.

Supporting the Topic Sentence

READ the paragraph below; then follow the directions.

> The Chesapeake Bay Bridge-Tunnel is one of the most unusual water crossings in the world. It is really a series of tunnels, bridges, and causeways. To allow large ships an open-water channel, two tunnels, each over a mile long, were dug deep under the bay. For smaller ships to pass under, a bridge was built near each shore. The remainder of the crossing is made up of three causeways, or roads, built on top of large pilings that were sunk into the floor of the bay.

1. Locate the topic sentence in the above paragraph. ....

....

2. What is the subject of the topic sentence (and therefore the subject of the paragraph)?

....

3. What is the dominant impression (or point being made) in the topic sentence?

....

4. Does each sentence in the paragraph support the dominant impression? ....

READ the following groups of sentences carefully and fill in the blanks that follow each group with the subject and dominant impression. Then write a strong topic sentence on the lines at the beginning of each group of words.

1. ....

.... No flower is as large. The rafflesia, found in the rain forests of Sumatra, often weighs as much as fifteen pounds. Its thick, bright petals can reach a diameter of three feet. The rafflesia has no stem and no leaves; it is simply one enormous flower.

Subject: ....

Dominant Impression: ....

2. ....

.... This buck-toothed rodent spends his nights and days building dams, lodges, and canals. In one night a beaver can cut down a tree that is six inches thick, gnaw it into six-foot lengths, and drag the logs to the bank of a stream where he wants to build a dam. When building his dam, the beaver uses his flat tail to sling mud and pack it tightly to waterproof his structure. He then builds a two-story lodge, his house, in the middle of the pond created by his dam. If he runs out of young trees for the raw material, he simply goes farther from home, digs a canal (which may be over 1,000 feet long), and floats the lumber to his construction site!

Subject: ....

Dominant Impression: ....

3. ....

.... This tree may grow as many as 320 separate trunks and well over 3,000 smaller branches. It is not the largest tree in the world, but it is certainly the most complicated. Its life begins when birds drop the banyan seeds onto branches of a host tree. The seeds soon sprout, sending long ropelike shoots from the branches downward to root in the soil. These shoots gradually thicken into hundreds of trunks. Eventually the tangled trunks can enclose a ground area of more than 2,000 square feet.

Subject: ....

Dominant Impression: ....

Adding Supporting Details

Successful writers support their main ideas (topic sentences) with details, facts, quotations, stories (anecdotes)—whatever it takes to bring their writing to life. When you write, make certain to use enough supporting details to bring your subject to life.

READ the bare-bones paragraph below and the list of supporting details, ideas, facts, and characteristics that follows. Select several of these supporting details and rewrite the paragraph so that the main idea is well supported.

Paragraph: I have a pet dog. He plays with me. After we play, I feed him his favorite foods. I think he has it better than I do.

Supporting Details:

Name/Type	Personal characteristics	Description
German shepherd	long, floppy tail	gray
Thumper	big, trusting eyes	brown
Hamlet	sandburs in his coat	speckled
Labrador retriever	goofy grin	rust colored
Wilbur	slobbers	black
Irish setter	whines	shaggy
Roger	thinks he's King Tut	motley
poodle		has tongue that
mutt	**Favorite foods**	feels like
Chopper	bones	sandpaper
Queenie	Jell-O	
Lhasa apso	peanut butter and	**Privileges**
	jelly sandwiches	doesn't have to
Habits/Pastimes	apples	brush his teeth
Frisbee	Alpo	doesn't have to go
sleeps on the sofa	dog biscuits	to school
swims in the pool	celery	has his own rug
fetch	corn on the cob	doesn't have to
hide-and-seek	air-conditioned doghouse	take out the garbage
sleeps in my bed	doesn't have a curfew	
chases cats		

after words → Using the same six categories, brainstorm a list of supporting details concerning a pet (or person) you know.

Writing "List" Paragraphs

Generally, writers create meaning in their paragraphs by stating important ideas and supporting them with different levels of details. (This is how you write paragraphs.) There are, however, other ways in which writers create meaning in paragraphs.

READ the example paragraph that follows. (Pay special attention to the beginning of each sentence.)

> Schools are asked to do far too many things. They are asked to provide meals for their students. They are asked to provide counseling for those students who need advice and guidance. They are asked to provide health care for those individuals who require medical attention. They are asked to provide a wide variety of programs to meet the special needs of students. They are asked to provide extracurricular activities. And, in addition to all of this, schools are asked to provide quality instruction for all.

As you probably noted, each sentence in this paragraph begins with "Schools are asked . . ." or "They are asked . . . . " In addition, each sentence in the body of the paragraph expresses a single important idea. There are no follow-up details. In essence, this paragraph consists of a list of related and equally important ideas. It results in an effective piece of writing with a strong, clear message.

LIST 'N' WRITE: On your own paper, write a "list" paragraph, using the example above as your guide. Make sure the sentences in your paragraph basically start in the same way and say something of equal importance. (The open-ended sentences that follow provide possible starting points for your paragraph.)

- Students really care about . . .

- Music is . . .

- We need to clean up . . .

- Money is . . .

- Grandparents are . . .

- Sports are . . .

- *A topic of your own choosing*

after words → Share your list paragraph with a classmate. Those paragraphs that really work should be shared with the entire class.

Writing "Piggyback"

In the last activity, you learned about "list" paragraphs. (In case you forgot, each sentence in the body of a list paragraph is independent and of equal importance.) Quite a different pattern is established in a "piggyback" paragraph. The sentences all say something equally important, but they are dependent on what is said before and after them. Each sentence rides on the shoulders of its neighbors, piggyback.

- Graphically, a list paragraph looks like this:

    1 (A topic sentence)

       2 (Independent and interchangeable supporting sentence)

       2 (Independent . . .)

       2 (Independent . . .)

       2 (Independent . . .)

       2 (Independent . . .)

- Graphically, a piggyback paragraph looks like this:

    1 (A topic sentence)

       2 (Dependent supporting sentence)

         3 (Dependent . . .)

           4 (Dependent . . .)

             5 (Dependent . . .)

               6 (Dependent . . .)

READ the following paragraph, paying careful attention to the pattern of sentences. All the sentences in the paragraph naturally fit together. There is no stopping to make certain ideas clearer with additional details. It's full steam ahead. Generally speaking, if you tried to move sentences around, the pattern would break down and create a lot of confusion.

     It was an offhanded glance at a college schedule of classes that got me interested in writing poetry. The schedule stated that a poetry-writing class was being offered on Tuesday nights during the fall. I started to think about all of the times I had students write poems, yet I did very little of it myself. For some reason, I suddenly felt this was wrong. I couldn't expect my students to really get into poetry if their teacher didn't talk and act from firsthand experience. I knew right then and there that I would become part of that class. I really had no choice.

WRITE a piggyback paragraph of your own, using the example on the previous page as your guide. (The ideas that follow provide possible starting points for your writing.)

Write about

- something you've come to appreciate (an object, a quality, or a person),
- something you've learned (a skill, lesson, or truth),
- something you've become interested in (a hobby, a sport, or an activity),
- *or a topic of your own choosing.*

after words → Share your paragraph with a classmate. Check each other's work to make sure that all of the sentences shoulder their responsibility.

Writing Explanations

Once you understand the fundamentals of writing a paragraph, you can move on to the next logical step—actually writing paragraphs. Being able to write a paragraph of clear explanation is an essential skill for every student. You will be called upon to use this skill in your classes for nearly every kind of task—from writing a summary to taking an essay exam. You will also be called upon to write clear explanations on the job—from an informal memo to a complete report. You will use this same skill often in your personal life—from writing an editorial to writing a letter of complaint.

READ the sample topic sentence below that could be used for a paragraph explaining how to take a good photograph. Following this example, fill in each blank with a subject that could also be used in a paragraph explaining how to do something.

1. Taking a _____good photograph_____ isn't all that difficult.

2. Building _____ can be fun.

3. Learning how to _____ is easy.

4. Planning a _____ can be exciting.

5. To replace a _____, you must take things one step at a time.

SELECT a topic from the list you just completed above (or add one of your own). State your proposed topic on the lines below. Then list each step that you will need to cover in your explanation.

Proposed Topic: _____

Steps: _____

_____

_____

_____

ARRANGE your steps into paragraph form. Use transitions as needed to tie your points together. Read what you are writing out loud and restate any part you think could be difficult to follow. If your paragraph begins to get lengthy, consider breaking it into two (or more) paragraphs. Make sure, though, that each paragraph contains a logical division or step in the process.

READ the paragraph below on washing a car before writing the final copy of your paragraph. Then, on the lines beneath the paragraph, list the things you would do differently if you were writing about washing a car. You may list errors, weaknesses, and problems that should be corrected in the sample paragraph; also list any other words, phrases, or steps you would add or change.

Washing a car is no easy process. First, you have to get a dirty car and a place to wash it. Then, you have to find a pail, a hose, and a sponge. Next, you should squirt the car with the hose. Next, you should put soap and water on the car with a sponge. Next, be sure to rub hard, especially on the dirty spots. Make sure you clean out the ashtrays, too. Leave the wheels until last because they are usually the dirtiest, at least most of the time they are, plus they are the lowest on the car. Next, wipe the car dry. Then, clean the inside of the car with a small broom or a vacuum cleaner. So you can see, washing a car is no easy process.

after words → Now go back to your own paragraph and finish revising and proofreading. Give your paragraph to a friend or classmate to read. Ask him or her to let you know where your paper might be confusing. Write your final copy on your own paper.

From Start to Finish

You should now be ready to handle a paragraph of explanation from start to finish.

CHOOSE a topic from the list below (or use a similar one of your own) for an explanation of a process or a machine and how it works. You will likely have to go to another source for your information. The challenge with this topic is to explain the process clearly and exactly, while at the same time making it interesting for the reader. (Be sure to put your explanation in your own words.)

- how a camera works
- how a census is taken
- how a VCR works
- how to purify salt water
- how to trace a phone call

- how a television works
- how to make a citizen's arrest
- how a lie detector works
- how a heart bypass is performed
- how a car is recalled

READ the sample below. Notice how the student who wrote this paragraph chose words that were more conversational than technical. Locate any five of these conversational words or phrases. Try to word your explanation in such a way that the average person can understand it.

Explaining a Process

Have you ever wondered how two people can hear one another so quickly and clearly when they are talking over the telephone? Actually, it's all done electronically and is really quite simple. When you speak into your phone, your voice hits a thin piece of metal—called a diaphragm—and causes it to vibrate. Right beneath this diaphragm are thousands of tiny carbon grains that are rearranged with each word you speak. The small amounts of electricity that are constantly flowing through your phone are increased according to what you say and how loudly you say it. These changing electric "pulses" move along the telephone lines and into the other phone. In the receiver of that phone there is another diaphragm; however, instead of grains of carbon, there is an electromagnet beneath it. As the electric pulses from the other phone reach the electromagnet, it gains in strength. As a result, the metal diaphragm is attracted to it and begins moving back and forth. As the diaphragm moves, it also moves the air surrounding it, creating sound waves that are identical to those created by the voice on the other end. The sound waves are picked up by the ear just as they would be if the speaker were in the same room as the listener. It's really quite simple, right?

WRITE, REVISE, & PROOFREAD your explanation carefully; ask a friend to read it over before you do your final copy.

The Expository Paragraph

When writing a paragraph, you can use two types of details as raw material for sentences supporting the topic sentence: **reasons** that explain **why** the topic sentence is true and **examples** that show **how** the topic sentence is true.

Both of these types of supporting details are commonly used in the expository paragraph. The purpose of the expository paragraph is to present facts about a person, place, thing, event, process, or issue. The expository paragraph explains its subject so that the reader understands it better.

READ & ANALYZE the following raw material that could be used in an expository paragraph. Write "topic sentence" on the blank before the sentence that would make the best topic sentence.

IDENTIFY each of the other sentences by writing "reason-why" or "example-how" on the blank.

.... **1.** The Black Death was so widespread because it was carried by fleas that lived on the large rat population of Europe.

.... **2.** The Black Death, which raged in Europe from 1347 to 1351, was the most devastating plague in human history.

.... **3.** The Black Death destroyed about one-quarter of the population of Europe.

.... **4.** Since today's antibiotics were not available, the Black Death, or bubonic plague, caused death in as many as 90 percent of those infected.

.... **5.** More than 75 million people lost their lives to the infectious disease.

READ the facts listed below about President James Garfield.

- James A. Garfield was born in a log cabin, like President Lincoln.
- James A. Garfield was the 20th president of the United States.
- James A. Garfield was ambidextrous, which means he could write with either his left hand or his right hand.
- James A. Garfield was a general during the Civil War.
- James A. Garfield is not one of our best-remembered presidents.
- James A. Garfield was unique among our presidents in being able to write two classical languages, Latin and Greek, at the same time, one with his left hand and one with his right hand.
- Latin and Greek have two very different alphabets.

WRITE a topic sentence for an expository paragraph about President James A. Garfield. Choose a dominant impression based on the facts you've just read.

Topic Sentence: ....

....

WRITE an expository paragraph about President James Garfield. Begin with your topic sentence. Create supporting sentences from the list of facts, but be selective and choose only those details that support the dominant impression presented in your topic sentence. Conclude with a strong summary sentence.

....

....

....

....

....

....

....

....

....

....

....

after words → Turn to the "Writing Topics" in your handbook and select a topic from the "Expository" list. Write a clear, creative paragraph on the topic of your choice.

Writing Business Letters

Why Write a Letter?

It doesn't really matter whether you use a computer, a telephone, a laser beam, or a letter to transfer your message: you are still the author of that message. But we all know that a telephone call is faster and more convenient than a letter, so why would anyone be concerned about knowing how to write a letter? Well, for one thing, faster and more convenient isn't always better. In the business world, for example, a letter has a number of very important advantages over a phone call.

Psst! Consider why and under what circumstances you may want to write a business letter. Maybe you are going to be looking for a job or requesting information about a college program. Your handbook gives you specific advice about writing business letters for a variety of specific reasons.

REFLECT: What advantages can you think of for writing a letter instead of making a phone call? Under what circumstances do you need to write letters? Have you ever written a business letter before? What were the circumstances? (Use the space below to record your thoughts or answer these questions.)

READ about the advantages of letter writing in your handbook. Look up "The Advantages of a Written Message." (Refer to "Letters, Business letters" in the index.) Compare what you wrote above to what your handbook has to say. If your handbook discusses advantages you didn't think of, write those advantages in your own words below. Share the results of this reflecting and recording activity. (Maybe you'll come up with some advantages we didn't think of.)

The Letter of Complaint

Above all else, there is one thing that you must remember about complaint letters: their purpose is not merely to complain. You write a complaint letter to get a problem fixed, not to whine, yell, or jump up and down on paper. If that's all you do, you might feel better in the short run, but you won't get your problem fixed.

DISCOVER: Find out what a letter of complaint should contain. Turn to the section in your handbook called "The Letter of Complaint" and read it over carefully. (See "Business writing, Letter of Complaint" in the index to find this information.) Then fill in the blanks below.

I should begin a letter of complaint with ....

and also include ....

....

When I have already ....,

I should explain ....

....

Finally, I should ....

....

AVOID: You should also be aware that there are certain phrases or expressions that come up over and over again in business letters. Most of these expressions should be avoided. Turn to "Expressions to Avoid in Business Writing" for a list of examples. (See "Business writing, Expressions to avoid" in the index.) Find at least one expression for each letter listed below.

a ....

b ....

c ....

d ....

Maggie Howard
212 West Walworth
Elkhorn, WI 53121
July 24, 1996

Customer Service Manager
Ed's Grease and Gears
123 Nutbolt Road
Delavan, WI 53115

Dear Sir or Madam:

I would like to register a complaint about a Spit & Sputter moped I purchased from you three months ago. I want fair compensation.

The floor model of this Spit & Sputter moped was very impressive, fuel efficient, and affordable. As soon as I saw it, I was sold. Your dealership ordered the moped a week later. However, I soon realized that something was very wrong. The moped rattles continuously and every time I try to go above 15 miles an hour, the engine kills. What's more, the moped has been burning oil and creating an unpleasant stench whenever I idle.

I tried to get this taken care of at your dealership, but the mechanics kept telling me it was the way I was driving. I finally took it to an independent mechanic and learned that the moped was refurbished, not new. I was shocked and feel that you must replace my moped with a new one.

I am assuming that you sold me a refurbished moped by mistake. I can give you a signed assessment from the independent mechanic proving the moped is not new, and then you can replace my moped. Please let me know how long it will take to get my new moped and if there is anything further you need from me. I will expect to hear from you within a week.

Thank you,

Maggie Howard

Maggie Howard

REVIEW the sample letter above. Working with a partner (if your teacher allows it), pinpoint and label the following information in the letter:

1. Product Information
2. Problem
3. Action Taken
4. Result Desired

PLAN a letter of your own in which you register a complaint about a recent purchase you have made. (This may be real or fictional.) Be sure to include all of the essential details related to the problem. Begin by filling in the blanks below:

Product information: ....

....

....

....

Problem: ....

....

....

....

Action taken: ....

....

....

....

Result desired: ....

....

....

....

FOLLOW the guidelines for writing a business letter and write the letter you have just planned. (You may use fictitious names, places, and dates, but make sure each part of your letter is correct and believable.) Before you write your final copy, proofread your letter carefully. Errors are simply not acceptable in business writing.

Proofreading Checklist

Form and Appearance

1. The letter is neatly written in ink or typed with no smudges or obvious corrections.

2. The letter contains all necessary parts of a business letter.

3. The letter is centered on the page, with spacing equal above and below and on left and right. Correct spacing is also necessary between parts of the letter.

4. The left-hand margin is exactly even.

5. The right-hand margin of the body of the letter is fairly even.

6. The signature is legible and written in blue or black ink.

Punctuation

1. A comma always separates the city and state. There is no comma between the state and ZIP code.

2. In the heading, a comma separates the day of the month from the year.

3. A colon is used after the salutation.

4. A comma is used after the closing.

Capitalization

1. The names of streets, cities, states, and people in the heading, inside address, or body are capitalized.

2. The month in the heading is capitalized.

3. The title of the person you are writing to and the name of the department and company listed in the inside address are capitalized.

4. The word "Dear" and all nouns in the salutation are capitalized.

5. Only the first word of the closing is capitalized.

Spelling

1. The numbered street names up to ten are spelled out. Figures are used for numbers above ten.
   Example: Tenth Street; 11th Street

2. The names of cities, streets, and months in the heading and inside address are spelled out. The state may be abbreviated, but make sure it is abbreviated correctly.

Writing the Thank-You Letter

Whether it's a handwritten note or a typed letter, a well-written thank-you makes people feel good and tells them you care about your relationship with them. Maybe someone did something special for you. She gave you crucial information for a project. He wrote a letter of recommendation for you. She granted you a job interview. When people do special things, thank them.

READ: You would think it would be easy to say thanks, but it can be tough to make your thanks sound real, yet not sappy. Fortunately, Victoria's letter gives us hints for doing it right.

June 5, 1996

Dear Ms. Applebaum:

I'm writing to thank you, as manager of Fresh-n-Ripe Groceries, for the excellent work of one of your delivery girls, Alberta Brinklemeister.

Yesterday afternoon she delivered my order precisely at 4:00 p.m., as I had asked. But she didn't leave the bags at the door. She brought them into my kitchen and helped me unpack! As a senior with arthritis in my hands, I really appreciated her help.

You're fortunate to have such a thoughtful and respectful employee. Even my cat Cleopatra, who uses most visitors as a scratching pole, loved her. I hope to see a lot of Alberta in the future.

Yours sincerely,

Victoria Regina

REACT: How does this letter demonstrate the following guidelines for writing a good thank-you?

Be prompt.

Be personal.

Be sincere.

Be specific.

WRITE: Say "thank you" by writing a letter to someone who's done something special for you. Here are some ideas for real or imagined readers:

- an eighth-grade teacher
- your guide on a field trip

Addressing the Business Letter

Addressing your letter correctly can be critical to the promptness of its delivery. The destination address must be exactly the same as the inside address, and the return address must match the heading. The destination address begins in the center of the envelope, and the return address is placed in the upper left-hand corner.

READ: Read the section in your handbook on "Addressing the Business Envelope." Then follow the correct form and address the envelopes to the people described below.

1. This letter goes to Vicki's Gondola House in the Boulevard Building at 1444 San Raphael Avenue in downtown Lavinia, Oklahoma 73848.

2. Miss Ethel Mueller is personnel director at the Grand Hotel on Orange Blossom Lane in St. Petersburg, Florida 33723. The number on the address you have is 333, but a recent mailing shows she has added P.O. Box 41 to her return address. Arrange the address accordingly.

Writing Summaries

The Summary

The summary is a brief statement of the main points in a text, expressed in your own words. In this shortened version, specific details and examples are not included. Instead, you stick to the general, overall meaning of the selection. A summary should give a sense of the whole rather than a detailed look at the individual parts.

You actually practice summarizing every day in interactions with family members and friends. When you relate what happened on your favorite TV sitcom or discuss the past weekend, you naturally provide a summary. You share the important points, the highlights, as they occurred. You use your own words and your unique style of expression.

SUMMARIZE: Write a personal summary of a famous fairy tale—*Jack and the Beanstalk*, *Goldilocks and the Three Bears*, *Hansel and Gretel*, etc. Remember to present only the highlights—a general story outline—in your summary. Also remember to use your own words and your own unique style of expression in your writing. (Use your own paper if you feel you will need more space.)

CHALLENGE!

Summarize one chapter in a book you are reading for enjoyment.

WRITE: Develop a one-paragraph summary of the "Sample Essay Answer" in the handbook. (Refer to "Essay test" in the index for this essay.) Make sure to present a sense of the whole essay rather than a list of specific facts and details as you find them. Also make sure to tie the important points together in a series of well-written sentences expressed in your own words.

Write a one-paragraph summary of the information presented in the introduction (the opening page) to "Listening Strategies" in the handbook. (Refer to "Listening skills" in the index for this information.)

The Index